TS-158
The
Professional's
Book of
KOI

Photographers: Aquarium Pharmaceuticals, Dr. Herbert R. Axelrod, V. Capaldi, Donald Dady and Eugene Krygowski, courtesy Eugene G. Danner Mfg. Inc., Dr. Guido Dingerkus, Dr. Bert Frank, Michael Gilroy, Burkhard Kahl, courtesy of Kamihata, courtesy of Lilypons Water Gardens, Fred Rosenzweig, Vincent Serbin, Takeshita, Edward C. Taylor, Van Ness Water Gardens, Wardley Products, Lothar Wischnath, R. Zukal. Photos on pages 24 through 26 dealing with pond construction are published through courtesy of Stapeley Water Gardens, Nantwich, Cheshire, England.

Artists: Scott Boldt, Richard Crammer, John R. Quinn.

Distributed in the UNITED STATES by T.F.H. Publications, Inc., One T.F.H. Plaza, Neptune City, NJ 07753; in CANADA to the Pet Trade by H & L Pet Supplies Inc., 27 Kingston Crescent, Kitchener, Ontario N2B 2T6; Rolf C. Hagen Ltd., 3225 Sartelon Street, Montreal 382 Quebec; in CANADA to the Book Trade by Macmillan of Canada (A Division of Canada Publishing Corporation), 164 Commander Boulevard, Agincourt, Ontario M1S 3C7; in ENGLAND by T.F.H. Publications, The Spinney, Parklands, Portsmouth PO7 6AR; in AUSTRALIA AND THE SOUTH PACIFIC by T.F.H. (Australia) Pty. Ltd., Box 149, Brookvale 2100 N.S.W., Australia; in NEW ZEALAND by Ross Haines & Son, Ltd., 82 D Elizabeth Knox Place, Panmure, Auckland, New Zealand; in the PHILIPPINES by Bio-Research, 5 Lippay Street, San Lorenzo Village, Makati, Rizal; in SOUTH AFRICA by Multipet Pty. Ltd., P.O. Box 35347, Northway, 4065, South Africa. Published by T.F.H. Publications, Inc. Manufactured in the United States of America by T.F.H. Publications, Inc.

The
Professional's
Book of
KOI

Anmarie Barrie

Contents

The carp, ancestor of today's fancy koi varieties, is a common motif in Chinese and Japanese works of art.

Introduction

The koi is the domesticated colored form of the wild common carp, *Cyprinus carpio*, native to slow-moving waters of Eurasia and the Middle East. Although it is the national fish of Japan, it is thought that the fish was originally introduced to that country from the lands around Iran. The first color mutations may have appeared there. It is the Japanese, though, that have been the main breeders of koi during its known history. Their skill and patience have produced the koi we know today. The finest koi in the world are found in Japan.

Of the many species of coldwater fish kept in ponds, there is little doubt that the koi reigns supreme. The koi is an animal of beautiful proportions and one of the world's most hardy fishes. Its limitless range of color patterns is the prime reason people are attracted to these fish. To see a mixed collection of top quality koi can be described as awe-inspiring. It is no wonder that some koi sell for as much as a new car. Not all koi are so highly priced; the average pondkeeper can purchase attractive specimens for prices which reflect the size and color

"Of the many species of coldwater fish kept in ponds, there is little doubt that the koi reigns supreme."

7

A 250-year-old Chinese vase—made during the Manchu dynasty—decorated with carp.

"Great age has been claimed for koi. Lifespans of 100 years and more have been attributed to Japanese specimens."

SIZE AND AGE

Koi may attain a length of 100 cm (39 in) and weigh in excess of 10 kg (22 lbs); such fish are rare, though. A length of 70 cm (27½ in) is possible in a large pond. Since koi grow extremely fast, they may reach 60 cm (24 in) under ideal conditions by the time they are four or five years old. Initially, growth is in length. As the fish nears its maximum size it increases its girth. It is possible for two similar sized koi to have greatly differing weights. Color may be linked to size as well; the largest fish are invariably of the most well-established colors.

Koi are larger than goldfish and more dorso-ventrally flattened. They are distinguished easily from goldfish by the presence of barbels. The mouth is less terminal and directed downwards.

Great age has been claimed for koi. Lifespans of 100 years and more have been attributed to Japanese specimens. The average koi is doing well if it lives past 20.

quality of these fish.

When Japanese is translated into English, it is possible for words to be spelled in two ways. In many cases "koi" is called "goi." Either is correct. The Japanese refer to carp as goi or koi; the color red is hi. Thus higoi is a red carp. Likewise, nishiki means colored—so another popular name is nishiki–goi. A less used name is irogoi, but the term stem is used for color feeding—iroage. Koi is the most popular name for collectively describing these fish.

EARLY HISTORY

Breeders of a domesticated animal species always lay claim to great antiquity. Koi breeders are no exception.

Many claim that these fish were bred as far back as 500 A.D. A more realistic date seems to be from the Middle Ages if you examine Japanese and Chinese art. Other authorities claim that breeding first commenced from mutations noticed during the early 19th century. This seems in keeping with the dramatic growth in the breeding of animal varieties generally. It is reasonable to suppose that, while koi may have been bred for centuries, selective breeding is a relatively recent happening.

By the turn of the century, koi were well established in many color patterns. The process of developing these patterns continues today.

Although koi have been pets of the Japanese for many years, it was only after World War II that Western countries took an interest.

During the 1960s the Japanese sent many more fish to international exhibitions. As this was a period of prosperity in the West, the beginning of a koi boom was heralded. Koi are now bred on a commercial scale in many countries, including Israel, Singapore, the U.S.A., Italy, Hong Kong and Great Britain. The biggest producer remains the Japanese. The Americans are their closest rivals for quantities. Germany produces fine koi, but it will be many years before they can rival top Japanese breeders.

"Breeders of a domesticated animal species always lay claim to great antiquity. Koi breeders are no exception."

The common carp, *Cyprinus carpio*.

A hand-painted split bamboo calendar decorated with koi.

popular way of identifying color types is to give them the name of a place or object, such as a bird or a mountain. Yet another method is to name the fish after a district or town. This may not indicate that the fish was of that area, though it originally was thought to be so. Finally, certain forms are given the name of the era in which they were developed. Where crossbreeding has produced a new variety, the names are added, on a build-up basis, of the fish used in the color.

KOI AS PETS

Because they are large fish and ones that enjoy eating, you can train koi to eat from your hand. A number of fish will throng around your hand, each trying to be the first fed. You will get to know each fish by its differing characteristics. You may even give each a name.

KOI IN JAPAN

Though koi have become big business in most English-speaking countries, this is nothing compared to the situation in Japan. Koi are a complete industry in that country. Thousands of people derive their living from these fish.

Since space is at a premium in Japan, Western type

A hand-painted split bamboo calendar decorated with koi.

THE LANGUAGE OF KOI

Koi names follow well planned Japanese systems of nomenclature. The most popular Japanese name is that of a color. A second gardens are often forsaken in order to allocate space to ornamental water gardens featuring koi. These ponds extend right up to the sides of the home. The owners can watch the fish from their living rooms. In some cases, the pools continue under the floors so that the koi can be fed from within the home.

Koi are family pets. They are given as presents to friends who own pools. They have long been regarded as good luck charms.

Koi exhibitions are popular. They are big affairs in which substantial prizes are won. Only a few of the millions of koi bred each year become star exhibits. Those that do are greatly prized and change hands for considerable sums.

Koi that do not meet the standards required for pets are eaten. Initially, koi and goldfish were kept purely as a food source. Their development as pets was probably the result of color mutations appearing in food stock.

This book considers each aspect of keeping koi from the beginner's viewpoint. The text will enable the newcomer to establish a pond and to select, feed, and breed these fish. Enthusiasts are encouraged to make further study.

A Chinese ivory carving of a Japanese merchant carrying koi bound for the market.

In their natural habitat, koi coexist with a variety of water plants. This is water pimpernel, *Samolus valerandi*, a plant that thrives in brackish water.

Habitat

Water covers much of the earth's surface, yet it is surprising how little the average person knows about this environment. Such knowledge is important to koi owners because of water's effect upon the fish. Because water is an alien environment to humans, it is easy to think that simply providing it is suitable to keep the fish in a healthy and contented state. However, water is to fish what air is to humans. It determines how many koi can be kept in a given volume, how well they survive, how well they are seen and how well they develop their color. It influences breeding abilities and controls growth.

Thousands of fish owners subject their fish to foul conditions. They do not do so deliberately, but simply because they do not realize that poor conditions exist and are detrimental. Poor water conditions can be improved dramatically by a

Koi pond around a Japanese temple. The garden pond is the most common habitat of pet koi.

13

A few water lilies will greatly enhance your koi pond, adding a lovely natural touch.

"In its natural state water varies considerably in its properties."

number of measures.

Have a good sized exit hole through which polluted water can leave. An inlet introducing fresh water and air makes things even better. Facilities to remove feces make life more tolerable, also. The fish must not be overcrowded; the number of fish must not consume more air than needed for stable breathing. A control over the upper and lower temperatures is beneficial. And of course, remove any fish that appears ill to reduce the risk of disease spreading. The way in which air is introduced, debris removed and temperature controlled is what pond and aquarium technology is all about.

THE WILD HABITAT

In its natural state water varies considerably in its properties. There are areas on earth that contain water with large amounts of salts— the oceans and seas. Other waters contain few similar salts—rivers and lakes. The former are marine environments; the latter are freshwater. Fish have evolved to live in one or the other of these conditions. Just a few species can survive in both. Within these two broad categories are further divisions. For example, some fish prefer water of higher temperature than do others—thus there are tropical and coldwater fish.

Koi are freshwater, coldwater fish. Because they live in waters that alternate between warm to cold, they have evolved to cope with wide temperature fluctuations. The fluctuations must be gradual, though. For example, the temperature changes slowly in rivers as the year goes from summer to autumn, through to winter and spring.

Water starts its cycle as being very pure. It contains few dissolved chemicals as it falls upon cool, clean mountain tops. As it flows down the mountains, it passes over various types of rock. Some rocks are hard, others are soft. Depending on the type of rock it flows over, the water dissolves chemicals within the rock. These chemicals become a feature of that water. The number of chemicals in the water tends to increase as the water reaches flatlands. Its state changes as it passes over marsh or lands containing decomposed plant life.

Sagittaria, or arrowhead, is one of the most readily available plants—it can be found in most aquarium stores.

All fish need oxygen. One of the main differences between land-dwellers and water-dwellers lies in the medium through which oxygen is taken in.

"Fish need oxygen just as we do. The amount of oxygen in a given volume of water controls the number of fish that the water can contain."

Different fish prefer to live in waters containing a given amount of chemicals. Koi prefer roughly a neutral pH. They are extremely adaptable, though. They can survive in both acidic soft water or hard alkaline water within the limits likely found in an average garden pool. A pH below 7.0 is acid. A pH above 7.0 is alkaline.

OXYGEN

Fish need oxygen just as we do. The amount of oxygen in a given volume of water controls the number of fish that the water can contain. This is not normally a problem in the wild because the number of fish compared to the volume of water is comparatively small. The situation is reversed in the garden pond because koi are large fish and the pools are small in relation to fish size. Care must be exercised in how many fish are placed into the water. The amount of oxygen in the water can be increased in order to stock more numbers of koi. This is accomplished with a pump and aerator.

PLANTS

A variety of plants have evolved which live in water.

There are even more which are basically terrestrial but can live in water, also. Plants are an integral part of a water habitat; they extract harmful chemicals. They also provide food for many life forms, ranging from bacteria to crustaceans to fish—including koi. This means that plants do not fare too well in a koi pond because the fish uproot or devour them. Certain surface leaved varieties of plants are safe with koi. The fish use them as sun shades on hot, sunny days. Water lilies are the usual plants for koi ponds.

WATER DEPTH

Rivers and lakes differ considerably in their depths. This affects the feeding habits of fish. Some have evolved to feed near the surface, others at mid-water levels and yet others are bottom-feeders. Koi are bottom-feeders, so unless the water is kept clear of debris and excess algae growth, you might not see too much of the fish. The way around this is to build a pool that is not very deep over much of its area. It must be deep enough, though, that it does not freeze solid to the bottom in the winter. Another way to maintain water clarity is to limit the

"Rivers and lakes differ considerably in their depths. This affects the feeding habits of fish. Some have evolved to feed near the surface, others at mid-water levels and yet others are bottom-feeders."

number of plants grown. The water can be passed through a series of filters that enables you to control the amount of debris and suspended particles in the water.

By feeding floating food pellets, the koi can be easily trained to feed from the surface of the water.

WATER PREDATORS

Carp must contend with various potential predators in the wild. These range from fish-eating birds and

"Koi will gladly eat any fish or water inhabitants that fit into their mouths. If other fish in the pond are of a reasonable size, then the koi will not harm them."

organisms. Some organisms are not a direct threat in themselves, but they may be carriers of disease that could harm the entire population of koi in the pond. Because koi are brightly colored and the pools shallow, owners in areas of fish-eating birds must be on the look out.

Water is a complex habitat. The more you can learn about it, the better the fish will survive in it. The fish will be happier, healthier and give their owners more pleasure. The aquarist's object is to create water that contains just the right balance of microscopic organisms and bacteria to be of benefit, but water clear enough so that the fish can be viewed easily.

KOI SOCIABILITY

Koi will eat gladly any fish or water inhabitants that fit into their mouths. If other fish in the pond are of a reasonable size, then the koi will not harm them. Koi are slow moving fish, but they can display rapid bursts of speed when needed. They enjoy the company of their own kind and mix well with goldfish (goldfish are members of the same family—Cyprinidae). Koi also will coexist with many other coldwater species. Adding other species may

Hong Kong postage stamp depicting carp.

mammals to carnivorous fish, such as pike. Not all predators are large. Even small animals, such as the larvae stages of water beetles and dragon flies, kill fish fry. All predators are undesirable in a pool. The pondkeeper must be aware of and remove any potentially dangerous

highlight the colors of your koi. The darting movements of these other species in contrast to the slow movements of the koi add interest to a pool. Many owners do not mix their koi with other species.

Both koi and garden ponds are ubiquitous in the art world. Even Monet gives us his impression of "Water Lilies."

Koi and garden ponds were made for each other. The superlative way to enjoy these fish is to watch them in a pond of your own design.

Ornamental Ponds

After a long day at work there is nothing more restful than sitting beside a beautiful garden pond and listening to the gentle sounds of the water. The desire to find solitude has been a human characteristic for thousands of years. It is hardly surprising then that ornamental ponds have a long history indeed.

For many years the garden pond was strictly a feature of the gardens of the wealthy. The average man had to be content to visit the gardens of museums or public parks. The availability of cheaper and better materials, coupled with increased prosperity, has made possible a dramatic increase in the number of homes that feature garden ponds. It is not even necessary to have an

A koi pond in springtime. Note the tranquility evident in this panorama.

extensive amount of land. An attractive pool can be incorporated in a very small space. Petshops sell do-it-yourself kits for pond construction.

POND STYLES

Ponds may be divided into two basic types; formal and informal. The formal ponds follow geometric shapes. They are typical of those seen throughout the centuries in palatial gardens of Europe and the Near and Middle East. The pond had to blend with the architecture of the buildings built by the Arabs, Greeks and Romans. The pond would be featured in

courtyards with the focal point being either a statue, fountain or an archway leading to another walled garden. The style was simple and uncluttered. The pond enhanced the feeling of tranquility, but it was not the prime object of attention. It created just the right setting in which to admire the beauty of the architecture; it filled space without intruding on the vista of the surrounding buildings.

Ponds such as this became fashionable in Europe. They

fit in well with the neatly laid out lawns and flower beds which followed simple straight or circular lines and shapes. These ponds are still popular. They are ideal for any garden that is designed with clear, precise flower beds.

A formal pond may be sunk so that it is flush with the ground. Or it may be raised so that it is partly contained by a wall. Formal ponds are popular with koi owners because they are

ORNAMENTAL PONDS

simple to construct and practical to service. They can be placed close to the home. This means that the koi are attended and seen more easily.

The informal pool was developed in China, Korea and later in Japan. The idea was to reflect the natural world that these cultures wished to reproduce in their gardens. Oriental water gardens are places of great beauty that beckon you to stop, investigate, meander and enjoy. There is nothing to suggest that the pond is in any way organized. Of course such apparent beauty is the result of considerable planning to create just this illusion.

The oriental water garden does not rely at all on colorful flowers to create beauty. Many species of conifer, small bushes neatly shaped and stonework are used artfully. The stones are placed carefully on rising ground to create wonderful

"The informal pond was developed in China, Korea and later in Japan. The idea was to reflect the natural world that these cultures wished to reproduce in their gardens."

A koi pond does not have to be large to provide interest and enjoyment.

backdrops to the pool. The koi alone present the viewer with an array of bright colors. Stepping stones are placed in and around the pool so different views can be enjoyed. The art of bonsai is used to great effect in water gardens. Lanterns, bridges, teahouses and statues of birds or mammals enhance the overall design.

The informal pond is based on the concept of creating a sheltered haven in which the wonders of nature can be admired. The shapes of trees, the light and shade, the movement of water and the koi all are brought together in vistas of grandeur. All this is achieved in a comparatively small area by patient and devoted owners.

Although ponds normally fit into one of these two basic styles, it is possible to combine them. A formal pond can be built in an informal setting. However, exactly the right balance must be struck.

THE POND SITE

Both the fish and the pond benefit from direct sunlight, but some shade must be available. If a concrete pool is planned close to trees, it will not be long before the tree roots find their way to the pool and crack the concrete. If branches overhang the pond, they may release toxins into the water and shed leaves into it. Both are undesirable for the extra work they create in keeping the pond clean and healthy. Also, insects tend to congregate around trees and water. Have the pool as far from trees as possible; yet the pond should enjoy some shade. Study the movements of the sun and the shadows created at different times of the day before siting the pond.

In nature, ponds are found at the lowest level of a terrain. If your garden is sloping down away from your home, you can create an

electric and water sources, the greater is the initial installation cost of the pond. A pond situated close to the home has other advantages as well. The most obvious is the ease of seeing the fish.

Few Western owners have the pond extending into the home. It is possible to construct the pond so that it comes within a few feet of the house. A pond in this

artificial situation by building up a rockery behind the pool. The pond will appear to be in a low point of the garden. Excavated earth from the site can be used.

In a flat garden, both shade and windbreaks can be established in the form of quick growing conifers. Alternatively, you could erect a woven style fence. Or, you could combine the two.

The further away from

position is easily serviced and more conveniently connected to electric, water and sewage points. A sun shade can be constructed over all or part of the pond directly from the house walls.

A pond near the home must be kept extremely clean and healthy. An uncared for pond smells badly and is an eyesore. Bear in mind that a

to view as many ponds as possible to evaluate the different pieces of equipment and landscaping. Look through more advanced koi, goldfish and garden pond books for more ideas.

It is a good idea to join a koi society. You will be kept up-to-date with the latest ideas. You also may be able to visit local koi owners and get their advice. Other owners are useful contacts even after the pond is built and the koi purchased.

Hobbyist magazines often run koi articles, especially *Tropical Fish Hobbyist* magazine which is the largest in the world! *Rinko* is a koi magazine published in English in Japan. It is edited by Dr. Kuroki, Japan's leading authority on koi. Most shops selling koi carry one or both of these magazines.

pond is a rather permanent fixture.

The prospective pondowner must consider the project for some time. A good pond cannot be produced quickly. The set-up requires pumping and drainage facilities, laying of filtration pipes and possibly underwater lighting. Permission of the local planning board may be required. It certainly is wise

POND CONSTRUCTION

Opt for the largest size pool you can afford, even if this means that not much money is allocated to landscaping. Decorative features can be added at a later date. But once the pond is built, it is difficult and costly to change the size or shape, or to improve the facilities. Small ponds are more difficult to maintain and are more restricted in the size and number of fish that can be kept.

The surface area should be no less than 14 square meters (150 square feet). This allows you to keep at least 15 koi with an average length of 30 cm (12 in). This works out to a total length of koi (not including the tail) of 450 cm (180 in). When calculating the number of fish to be stocked, consider the ultimate size of the fish, not the size at the time of purchase. Otherwise the pond soon will be overstocked.

The depth of the pond can vary over its base from 45 cm (18 in) to 152 cm (60 in). The temperature of a pond that is too shallow fluctuates more rapidly. There is also the risk of it freezing solid in very cold weather if heating is not supplied. Even if you live in a warmer climate, it is advisable to provide some deep areas.

A raised pond is prepared more easily if it is of a formal shape. A raised pond has the advantage that you do not need to bend over to study your koi. However, it is not as natural in appearance, is more difficult to landscape and loses its temperature more rapidly than does a sunken pool. The sunken pond also offers greater scope to the enthusiast.

Materials

For many years the only choice for constructing a pond was concrete. Today concrete ponds are less popular due to the availability of poly vinyl chloride (PVC), butyl rubber and fiberglass. These materials are more easy to use, less likely to leak and more easily repaired.

CONCRETE is very strong and easily fashioned into any shape. It is also one of the cheaper options if you consider only the initial purchase price. Over time, concrete can work out to be the most expensive choice. It is subject to cracking as a result of temperature changes. Hair-line fractures are not readily observable yet can result in leaks. Concrete is the most permanent of all the

"A raised pond is prepared more easily if it is of a formal shape. A raised pond has the advantage that you do not need to bend over to study your koi."

Artist's rendering of an aboveground or raised concrete pool. Note the precast shell within.

When adding water to your garden pool, keeping the hose above the waterline will ensure proper oxygenation of the water.

"The first thing to do in preparing a sunken pond is to mark out the maximum surface area of the water."

materials. It has a long potential life if prepared with care.

PVC is an inexpensive material. It is also the most fragile; it is easily torn. Since its life potential is short, it is not recommended for use other than as a temporary water container. It can be used to line a bog garden of shallow depth and small area.

BUTYL RUBBER is the most durable of the synthetic materials. It can be fashioned to fit any shape; it takes the shape of the excavation hole simply by the pressure of the water on its sides. Butyl rubber is available in varying thicknesses. It has a long life expectancy. The better grades are guaranteed for twenty years or more. This material does not tear easily. Even if it should tear it can be repaired. The big drawback is the expense.

However, butyl rubber is recommended strongly to koi owners. Be sure that the material is suited to use for fish—some types of butyl rubber are manufactured using chemicals that are toxic to koi.

FIBERGLASS comes in two basic forms. The most popular is used to make pre-formed ponds of solid construction. These range in size, thickness, shape and color. Precast or molded ponds are usually too shallow. To have one of a suitable size may entail having a unit made to order. This is expensive. Overall, these ponds have unlimited life expectancy.

The second form of fiberglass is rendered into any shape using concrete, brick or wood. The material sets solidly, but the job is a tiresome one. Once set the pool has all the advantages of the precast units.

Preparing the Site

The first thing to do in preparing a sunken pond is to mark out the maximum surface area of the water. A series of wooden pegs joined with string can be used. A precast fiberglass pond can be turned upside-down and its outline marked on the ground.

If a concrete pond is

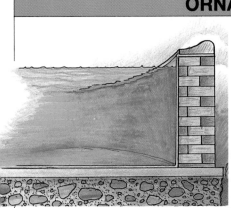

remain horizontal. A level and some string can act as a guide. The pond must be level across its width and along its length. If not level, water will overflow at one end while the liner or concrete is exposed at the other.

Excavation

Begin digging in the center of the site and work outward. Place the soil on the side that will be built into a rockery or other raised feature.

If the pond is of the minimum size, it is better that the sides be almost vertical. If it is of a large size, the sides can slope

planned, the actual surface area should be increased by at least 15 cm (6 in) to allow for the thickness of the concrete. (Add the same thickness to the depth, also.) Add an extra 45 cm (18 in) to the depth if a biological filter system will be incorporated.

If the site is on rising or falling ground, ensure that the surface area and the base

When constructing a concrete pond, especially one that is raised, be sure that the earth foundation is extremely solid and level.

PVC is becoming an increasingly popular material for lining garden ponds. It is highly recommended for use in small, relatively shallow ponds.

somewhat as there is sufficient depth to maintain an even temperature.

One or two shelves at differing levels around the edge of the pond can be used to support plants. The minimum depth for a shelf is about 30 cm (12 in). A shelf at another point can be 50 cm (20 in) deep. Their width should be 30-45 cm (12-18 in) if possible. Indicate these shelves on your plan so you remember where they are located. Shelves help animals escape if they fall into the pond.

Make a hole for a precast pond slightly wider and deeper all around. Allowance must be made for backfilling of soil to the sides. Also, a few inches of sand or fine soil should be used as a cushion on the base to allow for settling once the pond is filled with water. This is particularly important if the container is of the thinner and more flexible grades of fiberglass.

Once the hole has been excavated, it should be rammed down very hard at its base and sides. No stones, roots or other sharp protrusions should be seen that may pierce the liner.

It is not absolutely essential that a pond be fitted with a bottom drain, though it is certainly useful. A large pond may require two or more. A gentle slope toward the drains aids the movement

Placing paving stones around the edge of the pool and filling it with water are two of the last steps in pond construction.

A completed garden pool. Note how sparingly plants are used here.

of debris in their direction. Special drain units can be purchased for use with either concrete or liners. Since the drain outlet pipe will be lower than the pond bottom, a channel must be dug for this and filled over once the pipe is fitted.

The drain water may be sent either into a discharge box containing a standpipe or it may exit straight out of the pond to a suitable point. The drain can be controlled by a stop-cock. A lot depends on the overall layout of the pond and its surroundings in relation to other domestic services and waste removal pipes.

Be sure that the standpipe is slightly taller than the level of the water if the drainage is into a discharge box. When the pipe is lifted, the water will fill the box and exit via the discharge box outlet pipe to the drain system or into a dry well. The advantage of a discharge box is that you do not have to dig as deep in order to fit the piping to the eventual disposal point of the drained water. The drain sump can be emptied periodically by siphoning this with the aid of a mechanical pump.

Another excavation channel may be needed. This is a pipe taking the mid-level water to the filter system by force of gravity. The filter

"Special drain units can be purchased for use with either concrete or liners. Since the drain outlet pipe will be lower than the pond bottom, a channel must be dug for this and filled over once the pipe is fitted."

containers must be at pond level so that water discharges into the filter boxes. You may need to excavate for this. Whether they are placed near to or away from the pond is a matter of personal choice and practicality.

Although neither drains nor removal of water by gravity are essential (both can be equated by pumps) the extra effort is worthwhile for two reasons. First, you won't have to pay out money for electricity for something that can be achieved at no cost by letting gravity do the work. Second, the more that is done by natural processes the less that can go wrong during a power failure. The

one disadvantage of gravity systems is that they dictate the levels at which things must be placed. Filters can be sited more conveniently when the water is pumped.

There is one final piece of earth that should be removed once the total site excavation is complete. This is the earth immediately surrounding the pool. Since a pool is normally edged with slabs, the thickness of these slabs must be removed from the pond edge so that they are flush with the lawn. Slabs also hide the edge of the pond liner.

Liner Size

The size of the pond liner is the pond length + twice

the maximum depth + 60 cm × the pond width + twice the maximum depth + 60 cm. The 60 cm allows for 30 cm (12 in) overlap around the edge of the pool. Such dimensions will be more than your needs if the pond is other than a simple square or oblong. This is unavoidable. If you build an informal Japanese style pond, the planned shape will fit into simple oblong terms using these dimensions. If the pond is made up of two differing sized components, treat them as two separate units for purposes of calculation; the two can be

Garden pond in Kyoto, Japan. Most Japanese water gardeners prefer natural, informal pools.

silicone bonded together. When the liner is spread on the ground it may look enormous. It is quickly swallowed up as it takes the shape of the pond.

For example, a pond planned to be 3.5 × 4 × 1.5 m deep has a surface area of 14 sq m (150 sq. ft.). The lining needs to be 55 sq m or 594 square feet. As the depth is not 1.5 m over the entire pond, quite a bit must be trimmed. Maybe this can be used on some other small project. In the case of very large ponds, you may need to have a special liner.

CONCRETE PONDS

The foundation of a concrete pond must be extremely solid to restrict the movement and cracking of the concrete. A slight slope of the walls of concrete ponds reduces the risk of ice causing cracks in freezing weather. Shuttering or forming is needed to retain the wet mix until it hardens. Both the sides of the pond and the forms should be well watered or oiled before pouring the concrete, otherwise they will induce premature drying by drawing water from the concrete.

It may pay to rent a mini-mixer. The concrete mix should be 1 part cement, 2 parts sand and 3 parts clean, coarse pebbles. Suitable coloring agents and a waterproofing powder can be added.

Once the first 7.5 cm (3 in) of concrete has been laid, it is wise to include either metal rods or welded wire mesh to act as strengtheners. This is topped with another 7.5 cm of concrete. Pack the concrete well to remove air bubbles in the mix as it is placed behind the shuttering. It is better that the whole job is completed within 24 hours.

Score the top surface so that when it is dry a final coating of smoother concrete can be added. Once the concrete appears firm, remove the shuttering. Place damp cloths over the surface to slow down the drying rate. This ensures a stronger finish.

The lime in concrete is dangerous to fish. The pond requires a generous coat of sealant to prevent the lime from seeping into the water. Once the concrete has dried, it is wise to fill and empty the pond a few times over several weeks. Scrub the walls after each emptying.

A nice touch in concrete ponds close to the home is to tile them in an attractive manner. Keep the colors on the dark side. This way the full beauty of the koi colors

is not lost. The final test before adding koi to any pond is to check the pH. Introduce fish only when a reasonably neutral reading results.

Fitting Liners

Pool liners are easy to install and have no risk of polluting the water. They are safe from the moment they are fitted. There are two methods of fitting depending on whether the liner is PVC or butyl rubber.

PVC: Stretch the liner on

A striking fountain can become the focal point of your garden pond.

"The lime in concrete is dangerous to fish. The pond requires a generous coat of sealant to prevent the lime from seeping into the water."

"It [the PVC liner] must be tucked into the corners well so that there is no space between it and the pond corners. The weight of the water will tear the liner otherwise."

the lawn. Allow the sun to warm it for about 30 minutes. This makes the liner slightly more elastic. With the aid of one or two helpers, place the liner over the pond. Let it settle into the pond aided by a flat, but not sharp, weight. One person goes into the pond. From the center he smooths the PVC over the pond base. It must be tucked into the corners well so that there is no space between it and the pond corners. The weight of the water will tear the liner otherwise. The helpers work around the sides, smoothing the liner so it is as neat as possible. Add water via a hose. As the pond fills up, the sides can be smoothed further.

BUTYL LINERS: Stretch this across the pond. Weigh the edges down with stones. Pour water into the center of the liner. The liner will stretch and descend into the ground. As it does so, the retaining weights must be slackened every so often as the liner takes on the shape of the pool. Attach the drain sleeve once the liner is flat on the pond bottom. This process is continued until the pond is full.

To cushion the sides and the base, you can lay dampened sheets of paper or cardboard between the liner and the soil. Or, you can use the special padding available in stores.

Trim the surplus rubber once the pond is full. Leave a sufficient amount to extend beyond the pond sides. Secure the edges with slabs set onto a base of mortar for extra retention.

Petshops sell all kinds of liners and molded pools.

Raised Ponds

The supporting brickwork of a raised or semi-raised pond must be built on a very firm foundation. The brickwork itself should be substantial or of double thickness so there is no risk of its collapsing. Such a pond can be cement rendered, lined with fiberglass or fitted with a good quality butyl liner. The inner surface of the brickwork must be smooth.

DECORATING IDEAS

There are innumerable ways of making the pond and its surroundings beautiful. No doubt you have your own ideas. The suggestions here are given from a practical standpoint. It is better to plan for the decorations before construction is underway. This way any stress points created by the extra weight can be accounted for with reinforcement.

STEPPING STONES in regular or informal shapes always look appealing. They may be placed on the ground and in shallow water on a brick foundation. The sharp edges of the brick must be buffered. The best material

to use as supporting blocks for the stepping stones are breeze blocks. They are light and inexpensive. All items of a cement material must be treated as described for concrete ponds.

ISLANDS are easily created. They are excellent sites for small trees, conifers, lights or even a small sitting area. Earth or brickwork is made into an island before the liner is fitted. The liner is positioned as normal. The center is cut away and hidden at the edges. Lamp cabling can be run under the liner and into the island.

BRIDGES look good and give another vantage point from which to observe the fish. A bridge can be flat or slightly bowed. A lamp can be incorporated.

"There are innumerable ways of making the pond and its surroundings beautiful. No doubt you have your own ideas."

A carp pond in Hong Kong. Many pond owners incorporate oriental features into the layout of their pond. Bridges and rockeries are especially popular.

Opposite: A very natural effect can be created when a rock waterfall is incorporated into the pool.

"Care of the pond is not merely seasonal. Equipment should be checked regularly to see that it is working well. The growth and health of the koi must be monitored on a daily basis."

Garden pond in winter.

INFORMAL TABLES around the pool can be fashioned from old wooden telephone cable hubs or reels. These come in various sizes and can be gotten for virtually nothing. They can be painted black and trimmed with brass. The hubs can be made into tables or chairs. The hole in the center is useful for holding an arrangement of flowers or a sunshade. A cable can be brought through the hole to provide power for a lamp.

INTERNAL POND LIGHTING creates a stunning effect. Subtle lights add a touch of magic to the setting. Be sure that only fully waterproof fittings are used. I recommend the expertise of a qualified electrician.

FOUNTAINS should be used only in formal shaped ponds. They are not suited to intimate pools. This is better served by a waterfall.

SEASONAL POND CARE

Care of the pond is not merely seasonal. Equipment should be checked regularly to see that it is working well. The growth and health of the koi must be monitored on a daily basis.

The amount of seasonal care required in a koi pond depends on where the owner lives. When the temperature falls below 10° C (50° F), the

metabolism of the koi slows down. Below 6° C (43° F), the koi stay almost motionless on the pond bottom. Above 12° C (54° F), the koi remain quite active. They are most active when the temperature reaches 20-24° C (68-75° F). If you live in an area of long, cold winters, it is best to lift immature koi from the pond. Keep them in large, indoor tanks to minimize the loss. The young koi may not as yet have developed the fat reserve to tide them over a long winter without food.

Feeding

Koi consume the maximum amount of food at the peak of their activity. They build up their fat reserves to tide them over the winter. They continue to eat well even as the fall sets in, provided there are some warm and sunny days. The fish require little, if any, feeding during the winter. Excess feeding in the winter merely results in a build-up of decomposing food. Do not offer foods that promise not to cloud the water. All foods cloud the water if uneaten. Put some in a glass of pond water and smell what happens in only a few days!

Cleaning

Thoroughly clean the pond at the end of the summer. Take out all plants and remove dead leaves. Vacuum pumps can be used to clean the pond bottom. Clear drains of silt and debris. You may wish to cover the pond with a plastic mesh to keep out falling leaves.

If it gets very cold in your region, it may be wise to cover about two-thirds of the pond with good quality sheeting. This prevents the water temperature from

falling so drastically.

Make an air hole in the ice if the pond freezes over. *Do not use a hammer*. Either stand a pan of hot water on the ice until it melts, or purchase a pool heater. Such a heater consumes very little electricity. The idea is not to heat the whole pond, but just enough of an area to keep an air hole open. The air hole is not an absolute necessity, but it may trap poisonous gases, by-products of bacterial action, which can be forced to dissolve in the water, like soda water!

Filtration

The filter system must be at peak performance during the summer. This is when plants, fish and micro-organisms are all their most active. The turnover rate of water through the filters can be slowed down as fall approaches and the physical

Filters designed to remove harmful chemicals and debris come in different sizes to handle varying filtration requirements. Photo courtesy of E.G. Danner.

"The filter system must be at peak performance during the summer. This is when plants, fish and micro-organisms are all their most active."

activity level declines. Keep the filter operating unless the water in the filter pipe freezes. The filter pipe should be buried deep enough to avoid freezing, though.

It is unnecessary to have the water circulating at the summer rate all year because the fish use only basic energy in low temperatures. Indeed, it is better to reduce the water flow during the winter. This keeps the bottom at a slightly higher temperature than if the water were circulated upwards as it is in the summer.

It may be worthwhile to

At the end of the summer, the pond filter should be slowed down as the rate of aquatic activity decreases.

to minimize the disturbance of the water.

At this time the koi may appreciate mini-shelters on the pond base. These are made by arranging bricks or placing a number of suitably-sized drainage pipes on the bottom into which the koi can swim. The shelters offer security to the semi-hibernating fish.

A small formal garden pool. Formal pools are characterized by their adherence to symmetry and the inclusion of formal fountains and other furnishings.

alter the position of the pump during cold weather if it is a submersible type. Place the pump close to the return pipe from the filters so it draws water into the filter system and returns it at the same area of the pond. This reduces the overall circulation rate. The returned water that was sprayed onto the surface during warm weather can be immersed during the winter

Warmer Climates

Carp have a winter rest period under natural conditions. If you live in a climate where the water does not approach freezing conditions, it is beneficial to improvise a method of reducing the water temperature for an eight-week period. It is not known exactly how helpful the rest period is. Since it happens in nature, though, it is assumed

A lagoon-like garden pond.

to be favorable. Of course, the change in the water temperature should be gradual. So, too, should be its return to the normal temperature of the pond. A black plastic sheet suspended over the pond usually suffices. Do *not* lay the sheet on top of the water itself.

Koi Health

The koi must be examined in the fall to determine that they are in fit condition to cope with the coming winter. Any ill or underweight koi are best housed indoors or they may not survive to the springtime. Most koi losses happen over the winter in cold climates.

Springtime

The first pondlife to show itself as the winter gives way is the micro-life. Both plant and animals of unicellular construction rapidly take advantage of the warming conditions to multiply at a dramatic rate. The result is a green coloration to the water and a green filamentous covering on the surface. The latter is removed by skimming. The material in the water slowly disappears as the filter rate increases. Also, as the koi become active, they feed on the micro-life.

Do not give the fish a feast of food abruptly. This will only be wasted. The fish

"The koi must be examined in the fall to determine that they are in fit condition to cope with the coming winter."

The exquisite natural layout of this pond looks like it could have been created by Mother Nature herself.

A lovely informal garden pool. The well-tended, marginal plantings enhance rather than detract from this Japanese garden.

"Springtime is a busy period for pondowners. Plants must be placed into position, the health of the koi checked and probably a few repairs made here and there."

slowly increase their pace of life in relation to the developing season. The feeding must commence accordingly. Only feed floating pellets. Remove uneaten pellets after an hour. A good floating food remains floating in still water for at least 12 hours. Test yours in a water glass.

Springtime is a busy period for pondowners. Plants must be placed into position, the health of the koi checked and probably a few repairs made here and there. The pond surroundings also need attention. Heaters and other winter aids should be stored

neatly after they have been checked and serviced.

Failure of many garden ponds is attributable to the fact that owners set up a pool without installing a system to ensure healthy water conditions. Mechanical equipment greatly reduces the service time of pondkeeping, but every pond requires some effort on the part of the owner. The reward of this hard work is the joy of owning a garden pond. It is extremely satisfying being the creator of a complete ecosystem functioning in a balanced state.

Aeration and Filtration

The natural conditions found in wild habitats must be duplicated to some extent in the small confines of a pond. The idea is to ensure that an equilibrium exists between the various living and non-living components in the water. The living and non-living have arrived at a suitable balance over millions of years of evolution.

It is essential that certain processes be in operation in order that a koi pond remains in a good state of health. This is impossible if you simply fill a pond with water and leave it to itself. Merely having a few fish and plants does not create a workable ecosystem. Fish in the wild do not live in the same water each day. The water is moving continually. Even in ponds, water soaks through the earth, evaporates and is refilled when it rains.

Fish require oxygen, as do plants and other organisms in the pond. The warmer the

"The natural conditions found in wild habitats must be duplicated to some extent in the small confines of a pond."

water, the less oxygen it contains. This is why fish gasp at the water surface on warm days in overstocked ponds.

Fish and other micro-organisms expel carbon dioxide as a by-product of breathing. They also release waste products. All this, together with dead matter and uneaten food, decomposes at the pond bottom. Ammonium compounds, which are dangerous to the fish, are produced. The fish die if the level of poison reaches a certain point.

Dirt and other debris fall onto the pond surface. This, too, sinks to the pond base. Here it decomposes or releases chemicals in a dissolved state into the water. Most of the chemicals are absorbed if there is sufficient plant life. The plants may convert some of the chemicals into food items

It is important to use a fountain type that draws water from the pond itself rather than from an outside source.

A variety of garden pond fountains are available at your local pet or aquarium shop.

for their own needs.

Decomposition is caused by anaerobic bacteria (non-oxygen breathing lifeforms). They release nitrites into the water. These nitrites are lethal to fish. However, they are converted to nitrates by aerobic bacteria (oxygen breathing lifeforms). The plants absorb the nitrates. This is known as the nitrogen cycle. Ammonia is one of the lethal by products of this cycle.

A negative cycle commences if there is more waste in the water than can be coped with by the aerobic bacteria. The amount of ammonia compounds increases as decomposing waste covers the pond bottom. The available oxygen is reduced. This kills the beneficial bacteria which need oxygen to survive. As these bacteria die, less compounds are converted for the plants. The ammonia

"Decomposition is caused by anaerobic bacteria (non-oxygen breathing lifeforms). They release nitrites into the water. These nitrites are lethal to fish."

CHANGING THE WATER

The least expensive way to maintain water condition and clarity is to have a 25% water exchange every other week. This removes a lot of suspended debris and dilutes dissolved gases and chemicals. It is a time consuming operation and is completely impractical if the pond is large. Furthermore, if the water comes from a tap, it invariably is chlorinated. The water must be left to stand for a day or so for the chlorine to dissipate into the air, or it must be sprayed in a fine jet to achieve the same result. Even then the koi might be subjected to a sudden, undesirable change in the temperature and composition of the water.

A better way of maintaining condition and clarity is to utilize a mechanical means. This important process can be adjusted to proceed at a slow and steady rate until the right balance is achieved. Your petshop has many

level increases. The process gains momentum until all life, other than anaerobic, vanishes. Actually, a natural pond experiences this same process, if it is not fed by a stream, to become a bog or marsh.

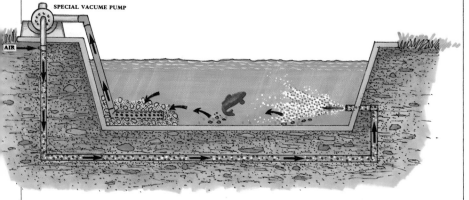

SPECIAL VACUME PUMP

AIR

pumps, filters and aerators to help keep your pond safe from stagnation and pollution.

AERATION

The amount of oxygen a given volume of water can contain is controlled by the surface area of the container. The depth has little importance except that it gives the fish more space in which to swim. The maximum oxygen content is in still water near the surface. This reduces in ratio to the depth. Thus the least amount of oxygen is at the bottom. Well-oxygenated water circulates to the bottom if currents can be created. The least oxygenated water rises to the surface to be replenished with air. The movement

A filtration system for garden ponds which works on basically the same principal as an undergravel filter in a home aquarium. A baffle filter is lodged in a pile of coarse stones. Small debris is bounced out of the water and into the rock pile due to the flow of air.

A fountain pump will increase your pond's capacity to sustain fish life. Some pumps also are equipped with lights. Photo courtesy of Hagen.

Above and below: Many different types of pond filters (such as the two shown here) are available on today's market. Be sure to purchase one that is suited to the size of your particular pond.

provides a more even spread of oxygen throughout the volume. A beneficial result is a more constant temperature throughout the depth; water tends to form distinct temperature layers if it is not circulated. Your petshop sells pumps to circulate and aerate your pond water.

A simple calculation determines the number of fish that a pond can accommodate. For every square meter (10.76 square ft) of surface area, 1.6 m (5.4 ft) of fish can be housed without additional oxygen being added to the water. This equates to the 155 sq. cm (24 sq. in.) that tank hobbyists use to calculate the number of centimeters (inches) of fish that can be contained in a coldwater aquarium. A simple example illustrates how many koi can be kept in a pond with

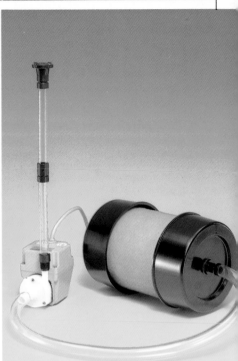

dimensions of 7 x 4 m (23 x 13 ft):

Surface area = 7 x 4 = 28 sq m or 301 sq. ft.

Number of fish = 28 sq m ÷ 1.6 = 17.5 m or 57.4 ft of fish.

Assuming that the koi will reach a body length (not including the tail) of 60 cm (24 in), then the pond can hold:

17.5m ÷ 60 cm = 29 m or 57.4 ft ÷ 24 in = 29 ft of fish

A pond of this size could take more than 29 ft of fish if they were at various stages of growth. Also, if the surface area could be increased, the number of fish the pond could hold would increase.

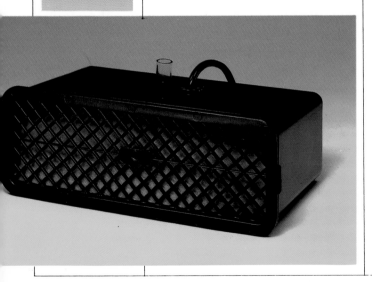

It is not necessary to increase the actual dimensions of the pond in order to increase its surface. Agitating the flat surface area creates tiny waves. These waves greatly increase the surface at which oxygen can be added to the water. Also, if the water is circulated so that it is taken out of the pond and then returned to it from a short height, this creates agitation and exposes the returned water to the air as well. The number of fish that can be accommodated rises dramatically.

The water can be taken from the pond either by gravity or a pump. A pump is still needed if a gravity system is used. The pump raises the water above the

pond height so that it can be returned via a waterfall or spray bars.

It is not possible to say just how many more fish could be kept. So many other factors need to be considered, such as the rate of water circulation, the extent of surface agitation, the temperature and so on. Even though more fish can be kept, you do not want the pond to look overstocked. Concentrate on keeping a reasonable stock that does not stress the system. Even if you do not keep the maximum number of fish in the pond, water circulation is still required to keep the pond clean. Aeration creates

A relatively simple fountain is best for a small garden pool such as this one.

Many manufacturers sell complete pond kits that include a liner, a filter, and a fountain. While you're at it, it wouldn't hurt to pick up a book about garden ponds.

even better conditions. Your local petshop can usually assist you in achieving suitable aeration.

FILTRATION

There are many ways of filtering the water. Since filtration makes the water more clear, the complexity of the system reflects the degree of clarity required by the pondowner for viewing his fish. Filtration removes unwanted suspended debris from the water. It also converts potentially dangerous chemicals into other compounds that will not affect the health of the koi.

The broad heading of filtration encompasses any method of removing unwanted debris from the pool. Certain processes technically are not filtration, but they conveniently are regarded as such since they make the water more healthy. These methods are mechanical, chemical and biological. It is normal for all three methods to be part of a good system.

A SIMPLE MECHANICAL FILTER: The water could enter the filter by the force of gravity if the tank is placed in the ground, near the pond, at the level of the water surface. Placing medium sized gravel or a layer of foam or plastic meshing in the tank helps filter the water of debris as it passes through. A pump could take the filtered water back to the pond. If this water was returned at a point opposite to the exit water hole, better circulation of the water would result.

The limitation of such a simple filter is that fine

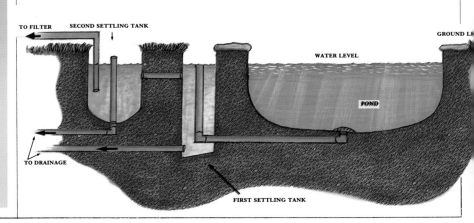

TO FILTER   SECOND SETTLING TANK   GROUND L

WATER LEVEL

POND

TO DRAINAGE

FIRST SETTLING TANK

suspended particles and dissolved chemicals would pass through. However, a very fine filter in the tank would clog quickly. The movement of the water through the medium would soon slow down dramatically. The solution is to place a number of filters placed near the pond and suitably disguised. There must be easy access to it for cleaning and replacing the filter media. Often pondowners use differing filters because some act as chemical filters as well.

CHEMICAL FILTRATION: A chemical

A fountain provides aeration by agitating the water, thus causing more water to be exposed to surface air. All aeration systems, including fountains, should be designed to work with the filtration system of a particular pond.

into the path of the water to remove debris in stages—the largest pieces first, then the smaller ones and so on. The filter chambers can be made of various materials, from fiberglass to marine wood or metal. This is mechanical filtration. All large ponds should have two or more mechanical filters.

The filtration system is filter medium converts ammonia waste compounds into inert chemicals and neutralizes other chemicals as well. Activated carbon chips and zeolite are the most popular examples. Both have excellent surface areas. They act both as mechanical and chemical filters due to their porous nature. Charcoal and coke are often used carbon mediums. If you prefer zeolite, this material can be reused. Simply immerse it in a saline solution for 24 hours. Thoroughly rinse it in freshwater and allow it to dry.

Because of the ability of these filters to convert the chemical composition of one compound to another, take care when medications are added to the pond water. These might be converted to other compounds as well, thus preventing the medicines from fulfilling their purpose. For this reason it is wise to have chemical filters in their own chamber fitted with a by-pass pipe. The need to turn off the filter system when the pond is treated with medicines is eliminated. It is a good idea to have all of the chambers of a large filtration unit arranged so that a by-pass system to each of them is possible. Cleaning, repair and replacement can be accomplished without disturbing the rest of the system, which can continue to operate as normal.

BIOLOGICAL FILTRATION: The benefit of biological filtration is that ammonia compounds are converted to nitrates that are relatively harmless to fishes. Such a system may be incorporated within a pond at the construction stage. This is internal or undergravel filtration. Or it may be achieved externally in chambers containing suitable media.

UNDERGRAVEL FILTRATION: An undergravel filter should cover at least one-third of the pond's base surface for the best results. It can be made by using strong plastic piping about 2.54 cm (1 in) in diameter. Make this into a frame by the use of 'T' and 'X' pieces, with 'L' pieces for the corners. One of the 'T' pieces is connected to the pick-up inlet of a submersible or external pump. Drill the piping with small holes about 65 mm (¼ in) in diameter. Space them about 15 cm (6 in) apart near the pick-up point and closer together as you get further away.

Lay the piping on the pond base on a few centimeters (inches) of large gravel. Cover it with a sheet of plastic meshing of a hole diameter small enough to prevent the top layer of gravel from falling into and blocking the pipe holes. Place a 23 cm (9 in) layer of gravel, 1.25-1.9 cm (½-¾ in) in size, on top of the base gravel suitably contained behind a solid wall. The pump will draw water into

"The advantages of an undergravel filter are many. This type of filter is hidden. It is also quite efficient if operating well. It is relatively easy and inexpensive to make."

the piping from the gravel. The water will be well oxygenated since it is drawn from the upper levels. The colonization of nitrifying bacteria will be encouraged to break down ammonia compounds on the gravel surface.

The advantages of an undergravel filter are many. This type of filter is hidden. It is also quite efficient if operating well. It is relatively easy and inexpensive to make. On the negative side, the filter must be incorporated at the building stage. Otherwise, the pond needs to be drained and may not be deep enough to accommodate a good depth of gravel. Depth is important for the success of the filter.

Medications added to the pond probably will kill the beneficial bacteria. The decomposed bacteria represent a serious threat to the fish due to the chemicals they release. However, modern medicines are available that do not harm the bacteria. Ask your petshop about them.

EXTERNAL FILTRATION: External biological filters are popular because they are more convenient and easier to control. The filter media are placed into containers through which the water is passed. The containers usually form part of a series of reservoirs, each doing a particular filter function.

The various media used are

For the most part, ducks and other aquatic fowl do not belong in the koi pond.

A very small tile type raised pond.

foam, processed lava granules, filter brushes, gravel and similar substances that provide a good surface area on which the bacteria can thrive. All these media double as mechanical filters as well.

Biological filters take time to become operational because the bacteria first must multiply to large numbers. Bacterial cultures can be purchased to speed up this initial phase. Likewise, small pieces of meat or fish can be placed in the filter chamber. Their decomposition provides food for the needed bacteria. Each filter comes with full instructions on how to use it. Ask your petshop to explain it further, and help you set it up, if you have any questions.

VEGETATIVE FILTRATION: Another method of biological filtration is to have a mini-pool filled with an assortment of plants. No koi are included in this pool.

Moat around the Japanese imperial palace. The bridge over your pond doesn't need a barbican to look great.

"There are innumerable ways to devise a suitable system once a basic understanding of aeration and filtration has been grasped."

The pond water is passed through this pool before its journey through the mechanical filters. The plants absorb nitrates and other chemicals. Periodic thinning of the plants is all that is required.

REFINEMENTS: There are innumerable ways to devise a suitable system once a basic understanding of aeration and filtration has been grasped. Some

This device restricts the flow of water in the outlet pipe. An air tube is connected to the outlet just beyond the restriction. The reduced pressure in the pipe at this junction creates a partial vacuum which sucks air from the standpipe into the outlet pipe. The water gets a good mixture of air before it enters the pond. Venturis can be purchased in a range of sizes. They have adjustable caps fitted to modify the rate of added air.

SIZE OF FILTER UNITS: It is difficult to be precise about the size of the filter needed in a pond. Many factors must be considered. A simple guide is that the total volume of the filter system should be no less than 10% of the pond volume. This size should provide good water clarity if the filter media are kept clean.

In a very large pond, especially in one that occurs naturally, the ecosystem will take care of the filtration for you.

pondkeepers pass the pond water into a settling tank. Large debris sinks to the bottom to be drained away periodically. The water proceeds into a vegetative filter and onto a series of chambers, each containing a different filter medium.

The amount of oxygen in the water when leaving the filter system can be increased by adding a Venturi tube.

PUMPS

Pumps are designed for either external or in-pond use. A few are usable in both situations. An external pump should be housed in a dry chamber where it is protected from wet weather, yet easily reached.

Choose a pump carefully because apparently similar units may have very different benefits. Consider the availability of replacement parts. Also, some pumps have comparable outputs yet their consumption of electricity varies greatly. Pumps are used to aerate or to push water through or pull it from a filter.

The output of a pump is measured in liters or gallons per hour. The average pond needs a pump that can move the pond's total water volume in about an hour. A large pond may be serviced better by two pumps rather than one. The test is whether the system keeps the water clear and the fish healthy. It is practically impossible to keep an outdoor pond crystal clear unless you spend an enormous sum for the system, or keep your pond small and shallow.

WATER TESTING

Periodically test the water, either at its return to the pond or at the point furthest from the returning pipe, to ascertain if the system is working well. Kits that test for nitrate, nitrate or ammonia levels, and pH can be bought from your local petshop.

The pH test measures the acidity of the water. The scale ranges from 0 (acid) to 14 (alkaline). Neutral is 7. Koi thrive between 6.5 to 8.

Substances of calcareous origin, like chalk and marble, raise the pH or make the water more alkaline. Peat and other vegetable or protein matter reduce the pH or make the water more acidic. Usually, acid water is soft while alkaline is hard. Your petshop sells kits for measuring water hardness, too.

A pH test kit is a necessity for maintaining proper water chemistry in the pond. Photo courtesy of Aquarium Pharmaceuticals, Inc.

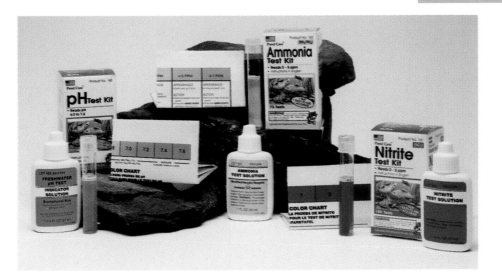

Plants

Koi and plants do not co-exist too well due to the habits of the koi in foraging the pond bottom. The number of plantings must be high and the number of koi low in order for the plants to survive. Then, the pond would be overgrown and the fish would rarely be seen. This defeats the purpose of keeping koi. For these reasons koi ponds are typically plant-free. A few selected lilies and a stand of rushes may be present. Many ponds in Japan contain no plants at all. Their scenes remain beautiful because of the superb surroundings alive with green trees and shrubs and various colors in the rocks.

If you still prefer to feature some plants, this can be done by carefully screening them from the koi. For example, a strong, plastic mesh fencing could be placed around some pond shelving. This can be used as a site for marginal plants. One or more small

Koi pond and environs planted with temperate flora. Don't plant tropical vegetation if you live near the arctic circle!

Opposite: Almost all ponds look better when their layout includes plants; however, resist the urge to overdo it. Too many plants spoil the pond.

islands can be incorporated in the construction stage. These are ideal spots for either bog, terrestrial or aquatic species.

Many aquatic plants do not thrive where the currents are strong. Site these plantings away from inlet and outlet water points. Plants featured in koi swimming areas should be protected by strong, plastic tubs or boxes. Cover any growing medium with a generous layer of medium sized gravel topped by small pebbles. This allows good aeration to the rooting

system, but prevents the koi from scattering the tub contents over the pond bottom.

WATER LILIES: These beautiful flowered plants of the family Nymphaeaceae deserve high regard by all pondowners. The genus *Nymphaea* contains those most generally sought. They have large, circular leaves which sport magnificent blooms in a range of colors.

Lilies can be various shades of white, yellow, pink or red.

There is an extensive range of cultivated hybrid forms apart from the wild species. There are so many hybrid forms that an attempt to list them is not practical. Visit a local water garden center to determine which varieties are available. Some companies specialize in water lilies. They produce color catalogues so that you can

on the surface of the pool.

Lilies prefer sunny spots. Do not place them near falling water or strong currents; swift moving water stunts their growth. The lilies provide shade under which the koi will bask on hot days.

The growing medium for

Artist's rendering of a waterlily, *Nymphaea alba*.

consider the flowers at your leisure. Some petshops sell water lilies, too.

When purchasing lilies it is important to consider their ultimate size. Some can become so large that they would dwarf a small pond. On the other hand, pygmy varieties look rather lost in a very large pond.

Some lilies grow in shallow waters of 23-30 cm (9-12 in). Others fare well in water up to 45 cm (18 in), while yet others prefer depths up to 122 cm or more (48 in). The deeper the water the more the leaves or pads will spread

"When purchasing lilies it is important to consider their ultimate size. Some can become so large that they would dwarf a small pond."

lilies is loam to which bone meal has been added. Trim off any dying leaves or roots. Place the plant in the loam so that just a tip of the tuberous rootstock is above the soil. Lightly hose the tub before placing it into the water to drive out air bubbles. You may need to place the tubs of deeper growing varieties on brick supports at first. The supports can be removed once the lily pads reach the water surface.

Planting should be done in the late spring. This ensures good summer blooms. The plants can be lifted in the late fall. Trim the dead parts

and store the rhizomes in a dry state. Lilies can be reproduced vegetatively by cutting the rhizome so that each segment contains a growing bud. Hardy water lilies can be left in the pond for a few years, but tropical lilies die in the winter unless they are removed. Charles Thomas wrote a wonderful book, *Water Gardens for Plants and Fish.* (TS-102; TFH.) Read it if you are interested in pond plants.

OTHER PLANTS: Members of the genus *Iris* provide delightful flowers in a range of colors. The purple-blues are especially attractive. The flower grows on a stem of up to 100 cm (39 in) from a rhizome. Plant them during the spring in shallow waters.

An appropriate plant for a koi pond is the *Lysichitum* which is native to Japan. It reaches a height of 90 cm (36 in) and sports a white spathe enveloping a green spadix. The plantain lily, *Hosta sieboldi*, also from Japan, is another good choice. The small, bell-like flowers grow on slender stems up to 90 cm (36 in) in height. The spear-shaped leaves are edged in white.

More suited to informal than formal ponds is the reedmace of the genus

Irises are popular due to their bright, vibrant colors and their lovely flowers.

A crop of wild irises.

Typha. A stand of these looks most natural to provide height at the end of the pond. They are characterized by their brown, tubular flowers which grow on long stems. These rampantly growing plants must be thinned down on occasion. They tend to be invasive, appearing where you don't want them. Choose one of the smaller growing varieties. These plants are often mistaken for bulrushes.

SUBMERGED PLANTS: The species most suitable for the vegetative filter are those

"More suited to informal than formal ponds is the reedmace of the genus Typha. *A stand of these looks most natural to provide height at the end of the pond."*

Artist's rendering of willow moss, *Fontinalis antipyretica*, a submerged plant.

such as Canadian pondweed, *Anacharis canadensis;* willow moss, *Fontinalis antipyretica;* arrowhead, *Sagittaria* spp; and water cabbage, *Samolus parviflorus.* These are hardy, strong growing and tolerant of a variety of water conditions. Other submerged

Water pimpernel or cabbage, *Samolus parviflorus.*

"The plantings around a pool reflect the individual taste of each pondowner and the style of the pond."

Artist's rendering of one of the reedmaces, *Typha latifolia.*

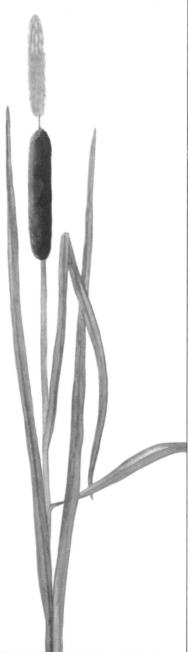

plants are suitable for a pond. A visit to your local koi dealer will familiarize you with an assortment of plants. Choose those which grow well in your region. These are well-suited to the climate.

POND SURROUNDINGS: The plantings around a pool reflect the individual taste of each pondowner and the style of the pond. Restrict your selection of plants and shrubs to those with good height. Create a setting that limits color to the many shades of greens. Western gardens tend to feature as much color as possible. Japanese gardeners consider this distasteful. It shows a

All irises do well at the edge of a pool—and they make wonderful bouquets.

Artist's rendering of one of the water pimpernels, *Samolus floribundus.*

"Conifers are hardy and grow in most soil types. A number have prostrate growth and so make excellent foreground cover."

Artist's rendering of one of the arrowheads, *Sagittaria guayanensis.*

acid soils, others require more alkaline conditions.

It may be impossible to feature the size of natural rocks that ideally should be included. Such rocks could require mini-cranes to set them in place. Artificial rocks can be made, though. Old bricks and rubble can be covered with cement that has

lack of appreciation of what beauty and nature are all about.

Visit reputable petshops to ensure that only healthy specimens are purchased. Avoid "cheap" plants because they are usually of poor quality. Conifers are hardy and grow in most soil types. A number have prostrate growth and so make excellent foreground cover. Bamboos and mosses can be used to create an excellent effect.

Allow sufficient space between shrubs for the growth. Check that the plants you choose are suited to the soil around your pond. Some plants grow well in

been treated with a coloring agent. A rock can be fashioned to the shape of sandstone or granite. Walls can be rendered as well to create a rock face. Boulders can be made by using fiberglass to cover a basic mesh of welded wire suitably shaped. These can be weighted with sand just prior to the final finish.

Small ponds of koi enhance this Japanese garden. Note the layout of the plants.

Despite the various color patterns it exhibits, the koi is still a carp at heart.

Anatomy and Physiology

The koi remains very much a carp from the anatomical viewpoint. It has some modification to the size of its fins and to its scales (and thus the colors it may exhibit). The koi is a typical coldwater species. It has evolved to survive ideally in many habitats.

BODY SHAPE

The koi is a long, elegant fish. It is more cylindrical in shape than its precursors. This is the result of selective breeding. The body is stocky and torpedo shaped when viewed from above. The widest point is between the pectoral fins and the beginning of the dorsal fin.

FINS

The fins of a koi include a large dorsal, a single caudal (tail), a single anal fin, and paired pectoral and ventral (pelvic) fins.

The dorsal is the major

"The koi is a long, elegant fish. It is more cylindrical in shape than its precursors."

71

The fins of the koi act as stabilizers as well as a means of propulsion through the water.

"The paired pectoral fins serve a number of functions. They are the main braking fins. This is achieved by the fish positioning them so that they provide a large surface area to the water."

stabilizing fin. It works much the same as the keel of a ship to keep the koi upright. It can be lowered to create a more streamlined effect when the fish moves at faster speeds.

The anal fin is positioned just forward of the tail, behind the vent. It is used essentially for stabilization.

The caudal fin acts as a rudder. It is the means for attaining maximum thrust by its good sized surface-to-water area. Its forked shape indicates the high speed capability of the koi. This speed is seldom used, though—only when the fish are frightened. The fish are quite content to move along with a sedate, easy-going style.

The ventral or pelvic fins

are paired. They are positioned about mid-body on the lower sides of the fish. They are used for directional changes. The fins act as hydrofoils as well, enabling the fish to rise or descend as it swims.

The paired pectoral fins serve a number of functions. They are the main braking fins. This is achieved by the fish positioning them so that they provide a large surface area to the water. They can be used to rotate the koi almost on its axis when one fin works in a direction opposite to the other. The action of the gills tends to create a forward momentum when a fish is motionless. This movement is counter-acted by the pectoral fins. These fins also are used to fan the substrate when the koi is foraging for food. Recently, Dr. Herbert Axelrod who wrote more koi books than anyone else, developed a strain of long-finned dwarf koi. These are more suitable for the aquarium than for the pond.

MOUTH

Some fish species have upward, or superior mouths. Others have terminal mouths—they face forward at the tip of the head. The mouth of a koi is placed in an inferior position. This means that it faces the pond bottom. The koi's mouth position indicates that it is a bottom feeder. This is further evidenced by the paired barbels on the upper lip. These fleshy growths are sense organs which help a koi locate food. But koi also rise from the bottom to eat floating or slowly sinking food.

GILLS

The complex gills have similar function to the lungs of higher vertebrates. They are protected from exterior damage by the gill cover, or operculum. Even so, they are still vulnerable to parasitic attack and fungal disease.

The gills are served by a series of fine blood vessels. When water is passed over the gills, oxygen is absorbed through the thin tissue of the blood vessels. This oxygen is transported directly to the body. Carbon dioxide and

"The koi's mouth position indicates that it is a bottom feeder. This is further evidenced by the paired barbels on the upper lip."

Skeleton of a koi.

other products of metabolism are released into the water via the gills. Waste solids and liquids are released through the anal pore.

Koi do not have teeth. They do have teeth-like serrations known as pharyngeal teeth. These are modifications to bones in the gills. They are situated at the back of the mouth, in the throat. They cannot bite you or hurt you when they take food from your hand.

EYES

The eyes are forward of the gills. They have no eyelids, thus giving fish their characteristic stare. Eyelids are not needed as the water itself acts as a lubricant to keep the eye clear of debris.

Koi can see in two directions at the same time— to either side of the body as well as above or below on each side. The fish have a

limited ability to focus on objects more than a foot or two in front of them. They have no great need for distance vision because other senses of the koi are far more acute.

NOSTRILS

Koi have nostrils just forward and slightly above the eyes. They are used purely as scent discriminators. The organs can detect hormones released by fish and other organisms. These scents either attract the koi or serve as danger signals.

EARS

Fish have internal ears that respond to vibrations in the water. There are no external or middle ears, so their hearing is not comparable to that of land animals. The auditory canal is concerned also with balance because it is connected to the swim or airbladder.

Artist's rendering of the interior organs of a fish.

LATERAL LINE

Along the sides is the lateral line of the fish. It is a series of pores in the scales. These connect to a channel under the skin which extends to the head. This channel is filled with a viscous liquid. The lateral line is especially sensitive to both vibrations and movements in the water. It acts somewhat as a sixth sense for the koi.

SCALES

The scales of a fish are formed early in its life. Once complete, they simply grow as the fish grows. Scales overlap one another and are transparent. According to type, the scales of koi may be larger than normal, smaller than normal or even absent. They also may be highly reflective.

COLOR

Color variation in koi has nothing to do with the scales. It is determined by the amount of reflective tissue, or guanin, in the skin below the scales. A fish exhibits metallic colors if this layer is complete. More colors are visible deeper in the skin if the layer is partially or totally missing.

The pigments found in koi are red-orange, yellow, brown and black. The red-orange is actually yellow modified by the effect of the hemoglobin in the blood. The differing levels of these pigments in the skin create

"The scales of a fish are formed early in its life. Once complete, they simply grow as the fish grows. Scales overlap one another and are transparent."

the magnificent array of colors displayed by these fish. Skin colors change rapidly during the first few years of a koi's life.

MUCUS LAYER

Koi have a layer of mucus covering the entire external form. This provides protection from potentially harmful lifeforms, such as bacteria and fungus. It gives fish their characteristic slippery feel. If the layer is damaged in any way, the koi may develop skin problems. These wound sites are prime targets for secondary invasions of bacteria which attack internal organs. This is why it is important for your hands to be wet when handling koi. This slime coating also keeps the koi from drying out if it jumps out of its pond and you find it quickly enough.

SWIMBLADDER

The swimbladder is situated just below the backbone. It is comprised of two different sized chambers which are modifications of the alimentary canal. Fish adjust their position in the water by inflating or deflating their swimbladders. The change alters their density relative to the water. The swimbladder controls the level at which the koi swim in the water. It also controls the orientation of the fish in conjunction with the auditory system. If either the swimbladder or the auditory system is injured or diseased, a koi may swim on one side, upside-down or at an unusual angle. It also may have difficulty rising to the surface, sinking to the bottom or maintaining a mid-water position. Swim bladder problems often are symptomatic of diseases, thus affecting the koi's ability to swim properly.

DIGESTIVE SYSTEM

Food entering the gullet of a koi passes directly into the intestines. Stretched out, the intestines are about four times the length of the fish. Koi have all the other internal organs you would expect: liver, kidneys, spleen, gall bladder, etc. All are concerned with the processing of food and expelling waste products.

REPRODUCTIVE ORGANS

Koi are not easy to sex because the sexes appear similar when they are not in breeding condition. The internal sex organs are the ovaries in the female and the testes in the male. In both cases they are located below the swimbladder. Eggs and sperm exit from the body via gonopores. These are connected to the gonads by the gonoduct. The gonopore is situated just behind the vent and just in front of the urinary opening.

NERVOUS SYSTEM

The brain of a koi is relatively simple. Optic and other sensory nerves radiate from it to the head. The spinal cord protects the central nervous system which extends to all parts of the body. Fibers at the nerve endings both receive and transmit messages to the brain.

LOCOMOTION

Fish move through water by alternatively contracting and relaxing muscles on either side of their bodies. The most powerful muscles are within the caudal peduncle. This is the part of the body just forward of the caudal fin. The result of the muscular action drives the tail fin side to side; the fish is propelled forward. The other fins correct sideway movements of the body. All this results in straight-line swimming. Changes in the angles of the other fins enable the fish to alter its course accordingly.

"The brain of a koi is relatively simple. Optic and other sensory nerves radiate from it to the head. The spinal cord protects the central nervous system which extends to all parts of the body."

The koi propels itself through the water by the use of muscles and fins.

A hi utsuri, or red and black reflection, koi. Any koi that you purchase should appear healthy, have all its scales, and should be swimming properly.

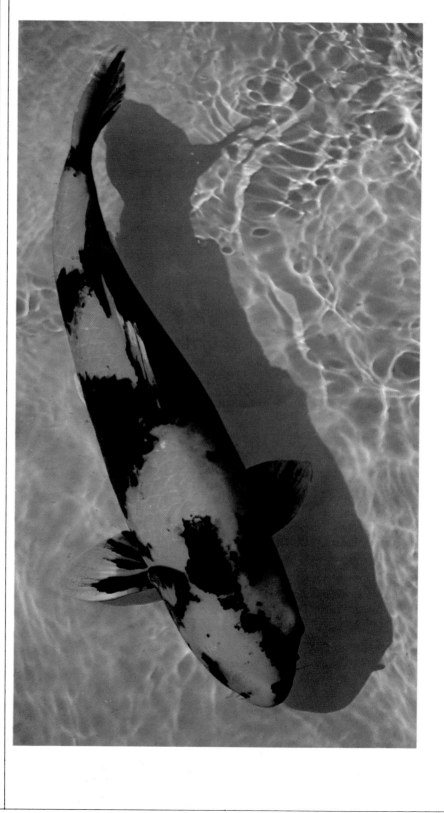

Selection

A prospective koi owner should exercise considerable care when purchasing stock for the pool. Koi are hardy fish, but they are vulnerable in the period preceding their arrival in a final home. Consider the changes the fish must endure during this period to appreciate the importance of buying koi from a reputable dealer. Also remember you get what you pay for. It's just as expensive and time consuming to care for an inexpensive, nondescript koi as a potential champion, colorful koi.

THE SELLING MARKET

Koi are bred in many countries, from the UK and Japan to Germany and Singapore. They are transported by the millions around the world in order to meet the demand for them both as ornamental and exhibition fish. Most koi pass through many hands before finding their ultimate home.

Koi are continually graded and transferred from one pool to another during the growing period of their lives.

They will have been moved on many occasions by the time they are one or two years old. Eventually they are sent to either major wholesale markets, or they are shipped across the world to importers. In the former case, the koi are placed in large stock pools. As buyers are found they may be shipped abroad. This constant movement stresses the fish. It is vital that they be well cared for at each stopping place by koi experts. The koi must be fully fit by the time they move onward in the selling market.

The fish are placed into quarantine tanks of the

Doitsu taisho sanshoku, or mirror tricolor, koi.

importer upon arrival. They then pass into the sales tanks or pools, if they are healthy, where the pondowner selects one or more. However, the koi may be purchased by smaller dealers. Once again the fish are shipped off and experience a quarantine period. It is unlikely that the water conditions exactly match at every change. This puts a great strain on the fish, too.

A good dealer devotes much care to the koi before resale to ensure they have no ailments. The fish should be feeding well. They should be housed in well-aerated, clean water. All this takes time and money. Therefore, it is not possible for a reputable dealer to sell koi cheaply. Those that do sell below market prices invariably have poor facilities, no quarantine period and keep overhead to a minimum. Purchasing from these dealers only invites disaster. You are not likely to get good specimens. Support only those establishments who have the proper conditions, and therefore the welfare of

"A good dealer devotes much care to the koi before resale to ensure they have no ailments. The fish should be eating well. They should be housed in well-aerated, clean water. All this takes time and money."

Shiro utsuri, or white reflection, koi.

Ai showa, or blue-speckled, koi.

". . .dealers can offer you sound advice. More than likely they will have a range of koi products and offer a complete service after purchase. They want your repeat business."

the koi as their prime concern. These dealers can offer you sound advice. More than likely they will have a range of koi products and offer a complete service after purchase. They want your repeat business.

TYPES OF DEALER

There are several types of reputable dealers. First, there are the koi specialists. They have an extensive range of koi, and maybe some other popular coldwater species as well. Prices range from the less expensive fish to more mature and highly priced individuals. The fish typically are displayed in under cover tanks or pools.

The second type of dealer is the more general pet shop that includes koi among many tropical fish for sale. These fish are suitable for the garden pond, but you are not likely to see exhibition fish. Limitations on space may restrict the number and sizes of fish that are offered.

PRICES

Koi prices vary considerably. Between the extremes are fish at every possible price. Finding one to suit your pocket is not difficult.

Prices are influenced by a number of factors:

1. SIZE. Specimens kept for longer periods are larger.

Beni goi, or red-orange, koi.

"Koi prices vary considerably. Between the extremes are fish at every possible price. Finding one to suit your pocket is not difficult."

In general, the larger a particular koi is, the higher its price will be.

"The better colored koi are more expensive. Single, double, and multicolored fish can be purchased. The placement and quality of markings must be considered, also."

In most cases, older koi are more expensive than younger ones. With an older koi, it is easier to tell the quality of its colors and patterns.

Their quality is more evident, thus the cost is greater.

2. ORIGIN. Generally, Japanese fish are more expensive than those bred elsewhere. Their colors are likely to be better. They probably have been bred along family lines. That is to say, they have been line-bred. Hence, they are more likely to pass on their qualities than those fish which are of unrelated breeding.

3. COLOR. The better colored koi are more expensive. Single, double and multicolored fish can be purchased. The placement and quality of the markings must be considered, also. There are other books, like Dr. Axelrod's *Koi Varieties*, which illustrate hundreds of champion koi. Check this book if you are seriously interested in koi.

AGE
The least expensive koi are the younger ones. They are one to two years old, ranging from 7.6 cm (3 in) to 20 cm (8 in). This is a good age to buy koi because you have the pleasure of watching them grow. Younger specimens may be purchased to be kept in indoor aquariums until they reach a size suitable for pond life.

HEALTH
Purchase only healthy koi. One ill fish can transmit disease to every other koi in

the pool. A good dealer will not sell you anything less than a healthy fish. Even so, thoroughly check the appearance of every fish you consider purchasing. Pass over any fish laying close to the tank bottom for any period of time. A motionless fish is likely to have a problem.

The salesperson will place your selection in a plastic bag half full of water. You can hold the bag up to inspect every side of the fish. There should be no torn edges on the fins, and no sign of missing scales, lesions, parasites or fungal growth anywhere on the body. The fish should be breathing at a steady rate. The eyes should be clear. It should have no difficulty maintaining an even keel in the water.

If a fish in the same pool as that of your selection is clearly ill, do not purchase any fish from that tank. Probably all the fish have been affected.

TRANSPORTATION

The bag in which the koi is placed contains air. However, if the journey home is long, ask the dealer

When purchasing koi, watch all the fish in a tank for signs of illness. If one fish seems sick, don't select a koi from that tank.

A trio of green carp, or koshi no hisoku.

"Although the pH of the water is not critical to the koi, the fish must not be plunged suddenly from one pH level to another."

to fill it with oxygen. It is helpful to place the bag in an insulated box to retain the temperature at a more constant level. Once home, the fish should be quarantined for three weeks before introducing it into the pond.

Although the pH of the water is not critical to the koi, the fish must not be plunged suddenly from one pH level to another. The

Hi utsuri, or red and black reflection, koi.

result will be shock stress. Ask the dealer what pH level the koi is used to and adjust the quarantine tank to this. The pH can be adjusted over the isolation period to equal that of the pool.

Do not release the koi into the isolation tank before letting the water in the transport bag equate that of the tank. Simply float the bag in the tank for an hour. If the bag was in a closed box, place cardboard or brown paper over the bag so the koi has time to adjust to the light. Now the fish can be transferred from its bag to the tank by lifting it out by hand or net. Do not allow the transport water to mix with the tank water.

Purchase the same kind of food that the dealer has been feeding to his fish. This can be changed slowly to your own regimen. The essential things at changeover periods

in a koi's life is that they are done gradually. The idea is to make the transition as smooth and stress-free as possible. Many health problems are a direct result of casual abuse. Many owners lack an understanding of sound fish

Yamabuki hariwake, or pale yellow white metallic with a gold pattern, koi.

When you first bring your new koi home, quarantine it for three weeks before placing it with other fish.

A pair of zuiun, or auspicious cloud, koi.

care and so cause problems and allow them to proliferate. Koi, though, are probably the most hardy of all pet fish. It takes a lot of abuse to hurt them.

Showa shusui koi, a mirror koi with blue, red, and sometimes black coloration.

Opposite: **Most koi are hardy fish. Treat them properly—feed them well (not too much!), give them suitable water conditions, etc.—and they should live a long, healthy life.**

Feeding

Koi are omnivores. They eat both animal and vegetable food. A good diet includes a variety of both of these matters. Fortunately, it is possible to purchase a wide range of commercially prepared foods. All koi foods must float for at least 8 hours. They must not cloud the water, if uneaten, for 48 hours. Test them in a glass. Don't believe label claims such as "does not cloud the water." All fish food clouds the water if uneaten.

THE ROLE OF FOOD

Koi metabolism functions on the same nutritional principles as do higher life forms. The food is utilized by the body for two basic purposes.

First, it is broken down into simpler compounds. A number of these are used as building blocks which enable

Proper foods and feeding will go a long way in keeping your koi healthy.

Opposite: Example of a healthy, well-fed but not-too-fat koi.

"The basic components [of food] are proteins, fats and carbohydrates. Add to these vitamins and minerals."

an animal to grow and to replace damaged or worn out tissue. Unwanted material, surplus to these building requirements, is used as fuel. Material not needed for fuel is either stored in the body as energy reserves (fat) or expelled as waste.

Second, food provides two basic forms of energy. The first is basic energy. This is needed at a more or less constant rate regardless of the koi's activity level. For example, the heart, kidneys, liver and other internal organs must be operational at all times. The second form of energy is needed to drive the fish through the water. This is muscular energy. It is required in considerably greater amounts than basic energy. It is also far more variable in its rate of consumption.

FOOD CONSTITUENTS

Some understanding of the constituents of food is necessary to appreciate their value in the diet. The basic components are proteins, fats and carbohydrates. Add to these vitamins and minerals. The final ingredient needed by all living animals is water. Its absorption and release from the body is as important to fish as it is to any other animal. Obtaining water is not a factor in keeping koi, but its quality is.

Proteins

Proteins are compounds created by the fusion of amino acids. Some are synthesized in the koi's body. Others, known as essential amino acids, must be provided from the flesh of other animals. This animal protein must be complete in its composition—thus the skin, muscle and internal organs of an animal must be offered for food. Commercial foods are formulated to ensure that this is so.

Proteins are contained in plants as well, but in small quantities. Certain amino acids are missing altogether. Furthermore, the digestion of cellulose from plants is more complex than that of animal tissue, thus it is a longer process. There are many reasons why animal protein is so important. Thus koi do not do well on a cereal-based diet.

Examples of protein rich foods are invertebrates such as earthworms, *Daphnia*, aquatic worms and insects. Meat, fish, eggs and cheese are also good sources. All proteins contain a high

percentage of water by total weight breakdown in their basic state. Commercially prepared proteins contain far less water. They may seem expensive, but far less of these concentrated foods needs to be offered to satisfy appetite than if protein were supplied in live animal form.

(Top) Daphnia species. These are considered one of the best foods.

(Bottom) Live Tubifex worms are eagerly eaten by koi, as they are by the *Corydoras* shown eating them here, but they are a potential source of pollution in the pool.

Carbohydrates

Simple sugars, or monosaccharides, are the cheapest form of fueling foods. These sugars combine to form more complex compounds, known collectively as carbohydrates. They are found in all vegetable matter. The amount of carbohydrates varies widely in differing

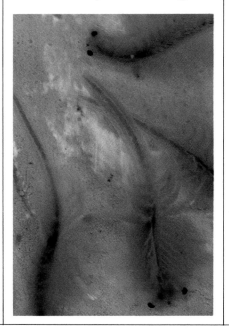

plants, as does the mineral and water content.

The most used form of carbohydrates in fish diets is derived from cereal crops, such as wheat, barley and maize. Household foods unsuitable for koi include bread, dog biscuits and breakfast cereals.

Fats

Fats comprise an important group of compounds. They may be liquid or solid in their physical state. Basic fatty acids are water soluble, but others are only partly so. Still others are insoluble in water.

Fats are often found in conjunction with proteins. They contain very little water compared to proteins. Fats are vital within the cell wall structure. Excess deposits are laid down to form an insulating layer which provides heat retention and acts as a buffer against knocks. In fact, fats are the most efficient form of energy, but they are a costly form. An increase in fats is useful for older koi. They find fats more digestible. Too many fats strain the liver and may lead to a fatal fatty liver disease.

Vitamins

Vitamins are required in comparatively small amounts

by fish. The effect, if any are missing, is quite marked, though, because vitamins are catalysts of chemical processes within tissue cells. Many vitamins are destroyed by heat. This is why the vitamin content of cooked foods drops dramatically. Commercially prepared foods are fortified after cooking, with vitamins likely to have been affected.

The richest source of vitamins is found in green plants, vegetables, fruit, liver and fish oils. A vitamin deficiency is unlikely if a range of plants and vegetables is included in the diet. Depending on the vitamin missing, a deficiency

A class of koi going vegetarian for a change. Many plants contain salubrious vitamins and minerals and should be offered to your koi.

"Depending on the vitamin missing, a deficiency can result in stunted growth, weight loss, inability to assimilate foods, loss of appetite, poor bone structure, loss of fertility, nervousness and general lack of health."

can result in stunted growth, weight loss, inability to assimilate foods, loss of appetite, poor bone structure, loss of fertility, nervousness and general lack of health.

While a deficiency is undesirable, an excess can be just as harmful. Not all unused vitamins are expelled. Some are retained within the body. An imbalance can be created which negates the value of other vitamins. Vitamin supplements, therefore, should be used with great care. Seek the advice of your pet dealer if you suspect your fish are suffering from a nutritional problem. Commercial koi foods, especially Japanese and American brands, are excellent.

Koi are easily trained to feed from your hand, and some will even come to the surface upon hearing their "name."

Minerals

The list of minerals, or base metals, crucial to fish is extensive. The amount required in nearly all instances is minimal. Thus they are often termed *trace elements* and expressed in parts per million. Typical examples are magnesium, cobalt, copper, zinc, sulfur, iodine, iron, fluorine, molybdenum and selenium. Two that are especially important are calcium and phosphorous. Calcium is needed in much larger quantities relative to other minerals. It is vital to the formation of sound bone structure.

Minerals are found in all foods as well as suspended in water. There is usually no need to provide them as separate items. The exception may be providing a calcium supplement prior to the breeding season.

Minerals form an integral part of the composition of all cells. They are used in many bodily processes; they are essential in the formation of vitamins. Minerals provide rigidity to muscles and bone. Any deficiencies show themselves in poor bodily structure and general lack of health.

Vegetables such as spinach, kale and lettuce are rich in

"The list of minerals, or base metals, crucial to fish is extensive. The amount required in nearly all instances is minimal. Thus they are often termed trace elements *and expressed in parts per million."*

and the body cells of a koi is considered.

The concentration of mineral salts within the body cells of freshwater fishes is higher than the surrounding water. Water is absorbed continually by body cells in an attempt to equalize the two. This process is osmosis. It is vital that water is also expelled in large volumes from freshwater fish. They would swell otherwise, getting bigger and bigger.

Koi release excess water through their gills and as urine. This may equal up to ten times their own weight every day. Clearly, any disturbance to the required concentration of minerals within body cells can have a dramatic effect on a fish's ability to release water. This will show itself by a fish becoming swollen and being unable to swim in a normal fashion. The owner may suspect that the fish has a swimbladder problem when it is actually plagued with a nutritional imbalance due to retention of water within the body cells. This disease is called *dropsy*.

A diet of high carbohydrate content is likely to result in just such a condition. The risk of feeding in an indiscriminate manner is reduced when an owner is aware of the importance of the composition of foods.

minerals and vitamins. So are many algal forms of plant life featured in commercially prepared foods.

BODY CELLS AND WATER

The importance of foods generally and vitamins and minerals in particular is illustrated well if the relationship between water

BALANCED DIETS

The overall menu should contain about 35% proteins of animal origin. The rest of the diet should be carbohydrates that provide energy. The amount of protein in the diet of young fish should be higher. Young fish grow rapidly and are more active. Fry require an almost totally protein diet. There should be no risk of protein deficiency at such a crucial stage of development. The carbohydrate content can be reduced gradually as the koi grow.

COMMERCIAL FOODS

Prepared fish foods have reached a high level of sophistication. They come in various forms, such as flakes, cubes, granules, pellets and powders. Some float for a while; others sink quickly. The floating types are popular with koi owners. These keepers encourage the fish to feed at the surface.

There are pellets for smaller koi, and both liquids and powders for fry. Frozen foods are available, too. Freeze dried foods are both convenient to use and store, and free from the risk of disease. Manufacturers of commercial foods offer different content ratios. Some foods have a high vegetable level, others high

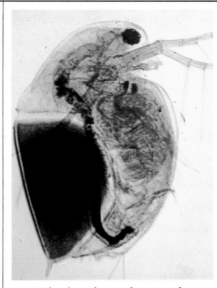

protein levels and yet others are multipurpose.

LIVEFOODS

The three ways of acquiring livefoods are by 1) breeding them from cultures supplied by pet stores, 2)

A representative species of *Daphnia.*

"Prepared fish foods have reached a high level of sophistication. They come in various forms, such as flakes, cubes, granules, pellets and powders."

A well-fed koi is seldom a sick one. Good food promotes good health, a high energy level, and maximum color quality.

"It is not vital for you to supply livefoods to the fish. Commercial preparations fulfill all their nutritional needs."

catching them in the wild, and 3) purchasing them from your local dealer. It is not vital for you to supply livefoods to the fish. Commercial preparations

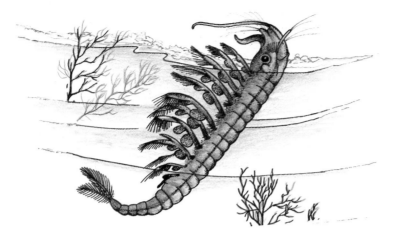

fulfill all their nutritional needs. The advantage of feeding livefoods is that uneaten morsels do not decompose in the pond. They live in the water until caught by the koi.

Collecting livefoods yourself is risky. Such foods almost certainly carry potential hazards, such as beetle larvae or disease bacteria, to your pool. Cultured foods are fine, but it is a tedious job maintaining the number of cultures required for koi.

Earthworms and maggots must be cleaned in freshwater or kept a few days in a sterile medium, such as sawdust or gardener's compost. The animals need time to clear their stomachs. Do not purchase maggots color-dyed for anglers. This dye may be toxic to your koi. Swatted flies can be fed to the fish—certainly not those killed with pesticide sprays, though.

The following are the most popular livefoods:

DAPHNIA: Also known as water fleas. These are tiny crustaceans. They may reach 5 mm in length. They

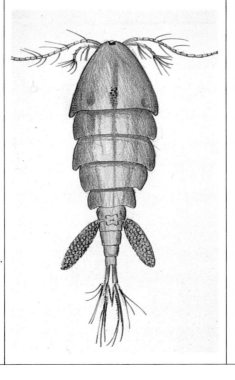

Hana shusui, or flower maiden mirror, koi.

"Frogs in a pond are beneficial. They consume various creatures that could be harmful to fry or carry disease."

Hageshiro, or black with patches of white, koi.

inhabit ponds and stagnant waters. *Daphnia* are enjoyed by all fish. They are good food for fry.

WORMS: An assortment of worms can be fed to koi. The most obvious is the garden earthworm. Another popular choice is red *Tubifex* worms. They are found in mud near sewage outlets. They grow over 2.5 cm (1 in) in length. They are available at most petshops selling fish.

GLASSWORMS: They are transparent and grow to 1.25 cm (½ in) in size. They are the larvae of a flying insect. These worms can be dangerous to fry, but they are eaten by koi more than a few inches in length.

BLOODWORMS: They are also larvae of midges. They grow to about the same length as glassworms. They are red in color and nutritious.

TADPOLES: Frogs may spawn in your pond. The tadpoles may be relished by the koi. Tadpoles of toads are ignored. Frogs in a pond are beneficial. They consume various creatures that could be harmful to fry or carry disease. Since certain frog species are endangered, do not remove spawn from natural habitats.

CYCLOPS: This is another small crustacean found in the same water as *Daphnia*. They are so named because of their

single eye. The larval stage is predacious and so not suitable for tiny fry.

INSECTS: Those suitable for koi include woodlice. These are found any place where wood is rotting. Winged insects, like grasshoppers, can be purchased from avicultural stores. Ask your petshop for livefoods which may not be mentioned here.

FEEDING TIME

Koi spend much of their time browse feeding, if plants are available, and foraging on the bottom. They take any livefood they can find. Many koi pools do not have plants or substrate. This restricts the amount of natural livefoods eaten. In such a case, it is better to feed the koi often, but in small amounts. This helps to keep them active. They should be fed at least twice a day—once in the morning and once late in the afternoon or early evening.

Alternate the food between largely protein meals and those with a higher carbohydrate content. Avoid offering the same menu every day. This way the koi's interest in meals remains high. All koi do not relish the same foods to the same degree. Individuals have preferred foods.

Koi owners should feed their koi when they are able to devote at least a few minutes to watching the fish. You will get to know individual habits of the fish. Note how much food is consumed and what types. A change of eating habits is often the first sign that something is amiss. It may even be worthwhile to keep records of everything to do with the koi. These records may be helpful in backtracking the source of a problem at a future date.

OVERFEEDING

Another benefit of observing your koi at feeding time is that you won't overfeed them. The problem is not really one of the fish becoming obese, but of polluting the water. Do not feed the fish more than they can consume in a five to ten minute period. Excess food eventually sinks to the bottom and decomposes.

"Koi spend much of their time browse feeding, if plants are available, and foraging on the bottom. They take any livefood they can find."

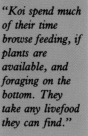

Hi shusui, or red mirror, koi.

Kin sui, or gold mirror (shusui), koi.

Colors and Terminology

Most popular pets were developed in the Western countries of the world. As a result the terminology is English. However, the language used for koi is Japanese. This is only fitting since the fish were established in Japan. This presents the newcomer to the hobby with problems because none of the descriptive terms are familiar. Each must be learned.

Many Japanese words, or parts of them, are combined to create other words and meanings on a build-up basis. Translation of terms varies somewhat depending on the authority, who may ascribe a slightly different meaning than the one intended in Japan. Even in Japan terms are not used consistently. Then again, certain words do not translate readily because a literal interpretation many have no meaning to a Western reader unfamiliar with the Japanese way of life.

BASIC TERMINOLOGY
The system of evaluating a

"Many Japanese words, or parts of them, are combined to create other words and meanings on a build-up basis."

"A koi is classified based on the number of colors it shows. This ranges from one to five. The way the colors blend and the density of the colors contribute to quality."

koi is really no different than that used with most domesticated animals. The major difference is the greater importance attached to color and markings. These are what koi are essentially all about. The overall shape is nonetheless important because the standard of quality in Japan is so high that often the shape is all there is to give a koi the edge over a similarly patterned fish. Swimming style is now gaining in importance.

A koi is classified based on the number of colors it

shows. This ranges from one to five. The way the colors blend and the density of the colors contribute to quality. The shape, number and placement of the color patterns are also important.

Colors in the Japanese language may be specific in translation—"hi" means red. Or they may be of a more complex nature derived from objects, such as the color of a bird or a bush— "yamabuki" is the yellow of a *Kerria japonica* plant. A koi may take the name of the place with which it was generally associated. It also may be called after the era—as in "taisho" (1912-1926)—during which it is believed to have been developed.

Other features of the fish may be indicated by the name. The scales of the fish may be of different types. Modification of the scales or any patterning effect of the colors all play their part in the Japanese system of koi nomenclature.

SCALE TYPE

The term *scale type* is somewhat misleading because scales are transparent. They are not responsible for coloration. Beneath the scales is a layer of tissue, the dermis or skin, in which the scales are embedded. This layer contains a layer of reflective tissue called *iridocytes*. Guanine is found within these cells. Above and below this reflective layer are chromatophores, cells containing pigments. These cells alter their shape depending on the mood of the fish and as a result of genetic influences affecting the chemical make-up of the cell.

The color of a koi is the end product of chemical changes within the chromatophores and of the changing shape of the cell.

The changes and shape alter the density of the pigments. In fact, pigment granules may disperse to differing parts of the cell which results in a patterning effect. The Japanese have selectively bred koi which exhibit such genetic mutations within the cells. Recombining these made possible the range of colors seen today.

Only the upper colors are seen in a normally scaled fish. The reflective layer

In addition to coming in various color varieties, koi are also available in different scale types or patterns.

prevents light passing through the outer, or epidermis, to the lower levels. Thus a normally scaled fish exhibits a high metallic sheen. Pigments deeper in the dermis are seen if part of the reflective layer is missing. Virtually all pigments are seen if the iridocyte layer is missing altogether. New colors apparently are created because some of the chromatophores are above one another, but at differing depths in the skin. A koi may have a reflective layer present in some areas but not in others. The fish then appears to have highly metallic colors where the layer is present. These areas sharply contrast with the dull areas where the layer is missing.

Typically only the part of the scale growing in the outer layer of the dermis, where it overlaps the lower level of the scale behind it, is seen. The outer edge of the scale grows as the fish grows. The number of scales remains constant. Four types of scales are recognized in koi:

1. NORMAL. Fully scaled fish which exhibit a high metallic sheen.

2. DOITSU. A number of scales are highly metallic while others have the reflective layer missing. This mutation was observed first in Germany. Such fish were

Gin kabuto, or silver helmet, koi. Note the scale pattern on the head.

called mirror carp. Examples were exported to Japan. They were incorporated into breeding programs to create an unusual and striking appearance in the fish showing this feature.

3. LEATHER. Scales are greatly reduced in size. The koi appears to be without scales, as the normal outer scale is absent.

4. GIN RIN. The scales display a mother-of-pearl sheen. This is created by part of the reflective tissue beneath a scale being complete while another part is thinner. The thinner tissue allows some of the light to enter the skin and not be reflected fully back to the viewer. It appears as a more matte color, but still with a dull sheen.

COLORS, PATTERNS AND MARKINGS

The following dictionary of koi terms will be useful. The fact that the Japanese have two or three words for a single color might seem to complicate matters at first. However, a word often tells more than just the color. For example, both "karasu" and "sumi" mean black, but the former indicates a totally black koi. The latter refers to a patch of black on the body of a two or more colored specimen. This is a recurring feature of Japanese terminology. The more fish you see, the more the system of names falls into a logical pattern.

"The fact that the Japanese have two or three words for a single color might seem to complicate matters at first. However, a word often tells more than just the color."

Aigoromo sanshoku, or red speckled with blue or black tricolor, koi.

"*Sanshoku is added to the term [aigoromo] if the black is quite distinct.*"

AIGOROMO—The red is speckled variably with blue. The blue is often very dark, almost black. Sanshoku is added to the term if the black is quite distinct.

AI SHOWA—A showa koi speckled with blue (indigo).
AKA—Red.
AKAME—Eye with a red iris.
AKEBI—Light blue.

Aigoromo koi; this fish has very small blue patches. This color variety is sometimes termed blue mantle.

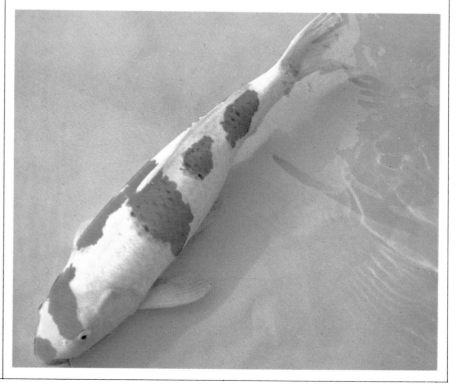

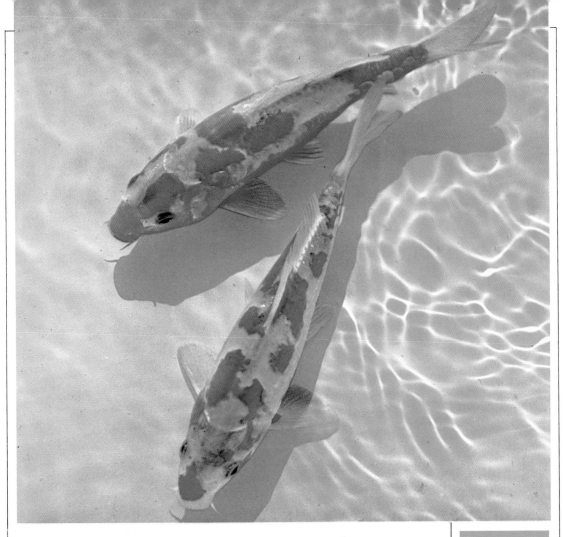

ASAGI—Blue. The term is usually applied to a koi with reticulated or pine cone patterns on the dorsal surface, red cheeks and a ventral streak of red that may extend to the pectoral and dorsal fins. The red may fade to orange or yellow. The shade of blue may be konjo (dark), narumi (mid) or akebi (light).

BEKKO—Tortoiseshell. This is slightly misleading. It does not refer to color, but specifically to the pattern. It means mottled. There are yellow torties with black, white with black, and red with black markings.

BENI—Orange-red.

BOKE—Faded color.

BUDO—An intermediate color between aigoromo and sumigoromo.

BUNKA—A variation of the tricolored pattern known as sanshoku.

CHA—Brown.

DOITSU—It essentially means *German*. It is applied to a koi having the striking mirror-like scales to the dorsal and lateral lines. Refers also to fish with no visible scales and of German

Tancho sanshoku gin rin, or red-patched tricolor gin rin, koi. Gin rin refers to the type of scales on this fish.

origin, but developed in Japan.

ENYU—A koi having doitsu scales of platinum which contrast with the red and white body color. Pale blue is interspersed with the

(Pronounced with a hard 'g' as in go.)

GOIOR KOI—Wild carp. Often abbreviated to goi or koi.

GOKE—A scale of a fish.

GOSHIKA—Five colors.

Kohaku, or red and white, gin rin koi.

"[The enyu is] A koi having doitsu scales of platinum which contrast with the red and white body color."

red and white on the dorsal surface. First bred in 1966. See also Raigo.

ETSU NO HISOKU—Basically a yellow-green koi of doitsu type. First bred in 1965.

GIN—Silver metallic.

GOTENSAKURA—A red and white koi (kohaku) liberally patched with red.

HAGESHIRO—Basically an all black koi (karasu). The head and snout are patched with white or brown. Small patches may be found on the

Shiro utsuri, or white and black, gin rin koi.

body and fins.

HAGOROMO—A variety of aigoromo.

HAJIRO—A black koi (karasu) in which the fins are edged with white.

HANAKO—The red

term stems from the word for cap or helmet.

KAGAMI GOI—A koi exhibiting the mirror-like scales of the doitsu. This is an old variety in which the mirror scales must be present

Goshiki shusui, or five-colored mirror, koi.

carp's pet name in Japan. It means "flower maiden."

HI—Red. (It is pronounced "he.")

HARIWAKE—White metallic with a gold pattern.

HISOKU—yellow-green coloration.

on both the dorsal and ventral sides.

KANAKO—Red-spotted on a white background. The name is derived from the white dappling seen in young deer.

KARASU—A totally black

"The name [kanako] is derived from the white dappling seen in young deer."

Kin kabuto, or gold helmet, koi.

INAZUMA—A zigzag pattern usually associated with the red and white koi (kohakus).

JIRO—White.

KABUTO—A koi in which the head color differs from that of the body. The

koi. It should have a velvet sheen. The fish often is tinged with a blue haze indicating their blue asagi heritage.

KAWA—A basically scaleless (leather) koi which has retained reflective scales

Kohaku, or red and white, koi.

"This [kohaku] is the most highly developed variety in Japan."

Menkaburi kohaku, or masked red and white, koi. Note the red head.

on the dorsal surface.

KAWARIMONO—Undefined color or pattern.

KI—Yellow. Not to be confused with gold.

KIN—Golden metallic.

KOHAKU—Red and white. This is the most highly developed variety in Japan.

KOMOYO—Small zigzag inazuma pattern of red and white.

KONJO—Dark blue. The precursor of karasu from asagi.

KOSHI—Green.

KUCHIBENI—Red-lipped. Derived from lipstick.

KUJAKU—Multicolored,

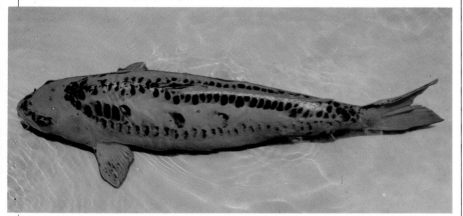

Mizuho ogon, or red golden metallic, koi.

as in a peacock.

KURO—Black.

MA—Wild.

MATSUBA—A pine cone or reticulated pattern. The center of the scale contains dark pigments. The edges are a lighter color.

MENKABURI—Masked. One of the many forms of the kohaku. The head is of a red color.

MEIJA—The era 1868-1912.

MOYO—Any patterned effect.

MUJI—Nothing else.

Applied to self or single colored koi.

NARUMI—Light blue.

NEZU—A gray or tarnished silver.

NIDAN—Two red patches on a white body.

OGON (OHGON)— Golden metallic. This may be combined with doitsu or matsuba patterns when silver or platinum ogons are produced.

ORENJI—Orange.

PARRACHINA—Very white metallic. Platinum.

RAIGO—A koi featuring blue, green and yellow-orange body colors, with bluish doitsu scales set on a black background. First produced in 1966.

RIN—A scale as in gin rin, silver metallic.

SANDAN—Three patches of red seen in the kohaku.

SANKE—A tricolored fish. Usually meaning red, white and black.

SANSHOKU—The same as sanke, a three colored koi.

SHIRO—White.

"This [ogon] may be combined with doitsu or matsuba patterns when silver or platinum ogons are produced."

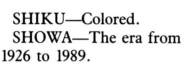

Tancho kohaku, or red-patched red and white, koi.

"This [shusui] is a mirror carp having a blue dorsal color with red on the ventral side. Much of the blue may be replaced by black in some variations."

Yamabuki ogon, or pale yellow golden metallic, koi; also known as the yellow rose carp.

SHIKU—Colored.

SHOWA—The era from 1926 to 1989.

SHUSUI—This is a mirror carp having a blue dorsal color with red on the ventral side. Much of the blue may be replaced by black in some variations. Produced during the Meija era.

SUI—A rippling effect, as in water. The colors have a slightly distorted look.

SUMI—A black patch or patches.

TAISHO—A tri-colored koi developed during the 1912-1926 era.

TANCHO—A red patch, ideally on an otherwise white body. Tanchos may be seen on other color forms providing that the red is visible only on the head. The shape of the patch is designated by various names, such as hato (heart-shaped), kakutan (square) or hinomaru (circle). The name comes from the Manchurian crane. This is a black and white bird sporting a roughly oval red cap of feathers on its head.

UTSURIMONO (UTSURI)—A black koi on which there is another color—red, white or yellow. Not to be confused with the shiro bekko, which is black patches on a white background.

YAMABUKI—Pale yellow. Named for the yellow petaled rose, *Kerria japonica*,

Ki utsuri, or yellow reflection, koi.

native to China.

YONDAN—A four patch pattern seen on kohaku.

YOTSUJIRO—A black (karasu) koi in which the head, fins and ventral surfaces are white.

YOROI—Armored. Usually applied to German carp which have more than the usual number of mirror scales, often irregular in their pattern.

ZUIUN—This is a color variant on the shusui theme. Here the doitsu scales are less evident and the blue more conspicuous as to form a wide streak down the upper dorsal sides. The tail is a soft shade of pink. The pink extends as a line forward of the dorsal fin. Black pigment may be more dense, though much reduced in area and extent, along the dorsal ridge.

"This [zuiun] is a color variant on the shusui scheme. Here the doitsu scales are less evident and the blue more conspicuous as to form a wide streak down the upper dorsal sides."

Breeding

There are few things as satisfying as winning shows with stock bred by yourself. Even non-exhibitors enjoy seeing fish in their ponds that they have bred and reared to their full magnificence.

Often a choice must be made between breeding and showing a fish. The problem is that the activities of the koi when breeding involve the male chasing and bumping the female. This induces her to release her eggs. Scales and fins can be damaged or lost during this courting ritual.

COSTS

It is possible to breed koi in a pool. However, few fry survive because the adults eat them. Koi do not exhibit paternal or maternal instincts toward their offspring. Furthermore, random breeding rarely produces the best fish. The objectives of

A long-finned koi; this variety was developed by Dr. Herbert R. Axelrod. Breeders are just now beginning to experiment with fin varieties in koi.

Opposite: Silk painting depicting a pair of koi.

> *"Although koi females release thousands of eggs, a large number of these are infertile. Many of those that do hatch fail to live, are of moderate quality or need to be culled."*

Showa sanshoku, or tricolor, koi. Always choose the healthiest and best-colored koi for breeding purposes.

nature do not always coincide with the desires of breeders.

This means that it is necessary to invest in additional breeding tanks where the adults can be placed for spawning. The adults are removed after spawning has taken place so that the fry can be reared in safety.

Although koi females release thousands of eggs, a large number of these are infertile. Many of those that do hatch fail to live, are of moderate quality or need to be culled. Breed only quality specimens. Mediocre fish produce mediocre offspring.

Do not attempt to raise too many koi from those that hatch. The fry consume more food as they grow. Larger rearing tanks, or more of them, are needed. Additionally, the breeder needs to devote a considerable amount of time to the fish. It is better to rear a few of a high standard than

Pond conditions should be as close to ideal as possible, especially if you want your koi to breed.

to underfeed the fish or overstock the facilities.

AGE

Do not breed immature koi. This results in less than vigorous fry. Only mature, healthy fish should be expected to reproduce. A female should be about two years old. A male should be an extra year older.

BREEDING PROGRAMS

Breeding success is the result of many aspects. No factor by itself insures success. The major requirements are as follows:

1. GOOD INITIAL STOCK. It does not have to

"Do not breed immature koi. This results in less that vigorous fry. Only mature, healthy fish should be expected to produce."

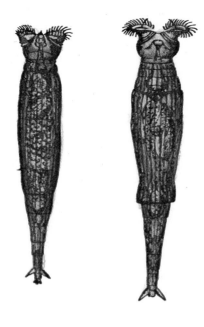

Artist's rendering of rotifers. These creatures make wonderful food for very young free-swimming fry.

Brown hi-fin koi. Note the elaborate finnage on this fish.

be top quality, as a breeder hopes to improve his stock over the years. The koi should have been produced from parents exhibiting good shape, finnage and color.

Markings should be as clean-lined as possible.

2. SOUND HUSBANDRY. Even the best koi can be ruined in the wrong hands. Quality

breeding means little if the koi are not kept in good water conditions and given a balanced diet. An overstocked pond limits development and breeding value. Good husbandry allows the fish to reach their maximum potential.

3. SELECTION. The hallmark of a top breeder is the ability to study and select the best fish. Indiscriminate breeding cannot create a steady upgrading of quality.

4. RECORD KEEPING. Memory fails over time. Written information allows for the sort of detailed comparison necessary in a breeding program. The more information you have about

Yellow hi-fin koi. Some hobbyists believe that hi-fins were created by hybridizing koi and goldfish.

Aka matsuba, or red pine cone, koi. Note the reticulated pattern on the scales.

the koi, the easier it is to trace problems and make improvements. Records should identify the individual characteristics of each fish bred. Note which fish have spawned with which, colors produced, number of fry, feeding regimen, illness and all other pertinent data.

reach breeding condition. At such time, females show abdominal swelling, often more to one side than the other. This is the result of the eggs developing in their ovaries. Males may exhibit small, white tubercles on their gill covers, face, head and pectoral fins.

PREPARATION. Separate

Yondan kohaku, or four-patched red and white, koi.

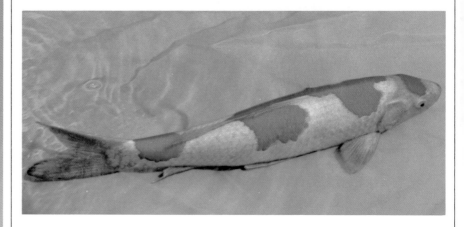

PROCEDURE

SEXING. Koi are sexually non-dimorphic when not in breeding condition; the sexes look very similar. Males are slimmer than females, have larger pectoral fins in proportion to body size and have larger head ratios. Females look plumper before spawning in the spring. They also grow larger than males.

These are only relative states and cannot be relied upon as a guide to sex. Differences only become obvious as the mature fish

"Koi are sexually non-dimorphic when not in breeding condition; the sexes look very similar."

the sexes in the fall after selecting the fish to be bred. By the time spring rolls around the fish will be eager to commence mating if the conditions are right.

A spawning tank can be a temporary or permanent feature. It should be about 3 m x 1.8 m x 60 cm deep (10 ft x 6 ft x 24 in). Add water matching the conditions of the pond. Place a suitable spawning material at one end. This may be spawning brushes, mops, branches of conifer leaves, water hyacinth or other water

Tancho sanshoku, or red-patched tricolor, gin rin koi.

Kohaku, or red and white, koi.

plants or mosses. The eggs attach to these materials.

SPAWNING. Place the koi into the breeding pool once they are clearly in breeding condition. Typically two or three males are placed with one female to ensure a high fertilization of eggs. More of each sex can be placed in a pool, but larger accommodations are needed as the fry grow quickly.

The courting ritual commences by the males chasing the female. The chasing becomes hectic. Eventually the female swims into the spawning area and

Gin matsuba, or silver metallic pine cone, koi.

Top: **Kinbo, or golden metallic, koi.** *Bottom:* **Ginbo, or silver staff, koi.**

Gin sui, or silver metallic mirror, koi.

"Spawning usually occurs early in the morning. Once complete, carefully net and return the fish to their normal pond."

Kin matsuba, or golden metallic pine cone, koi.

sheds her eggs. The males simultaneously draw alongside of her to release their sperm, or milt. Spawning usually occurs early in the morning. Once complete, carefully net and return the fish to their normal pond. It is not necessary to feed the adults while they are in the breeding pool. The food can create pollution not good for the fry.

HATCHING. Temperature controls the speed of hatching. The eggs hatch in four to six days if the temperature is around 22° C (72° F). Raising the temperature hastens the hatching; a lower temperature slows the rate. A number of eggs will not hatch, either because they are infertile or because the embryo died. These eggs shrivel up and are eaten by bacteria and fungus in the water.

REARING THE FRY

Fry do not require food for the first 36 hours after hatching. They gain nourishment from their egg sac. Feeding begins when the fry are free-swimming.

FEEDING. Favored foods are *Daphnia* and proprietary powdered foods. Food must

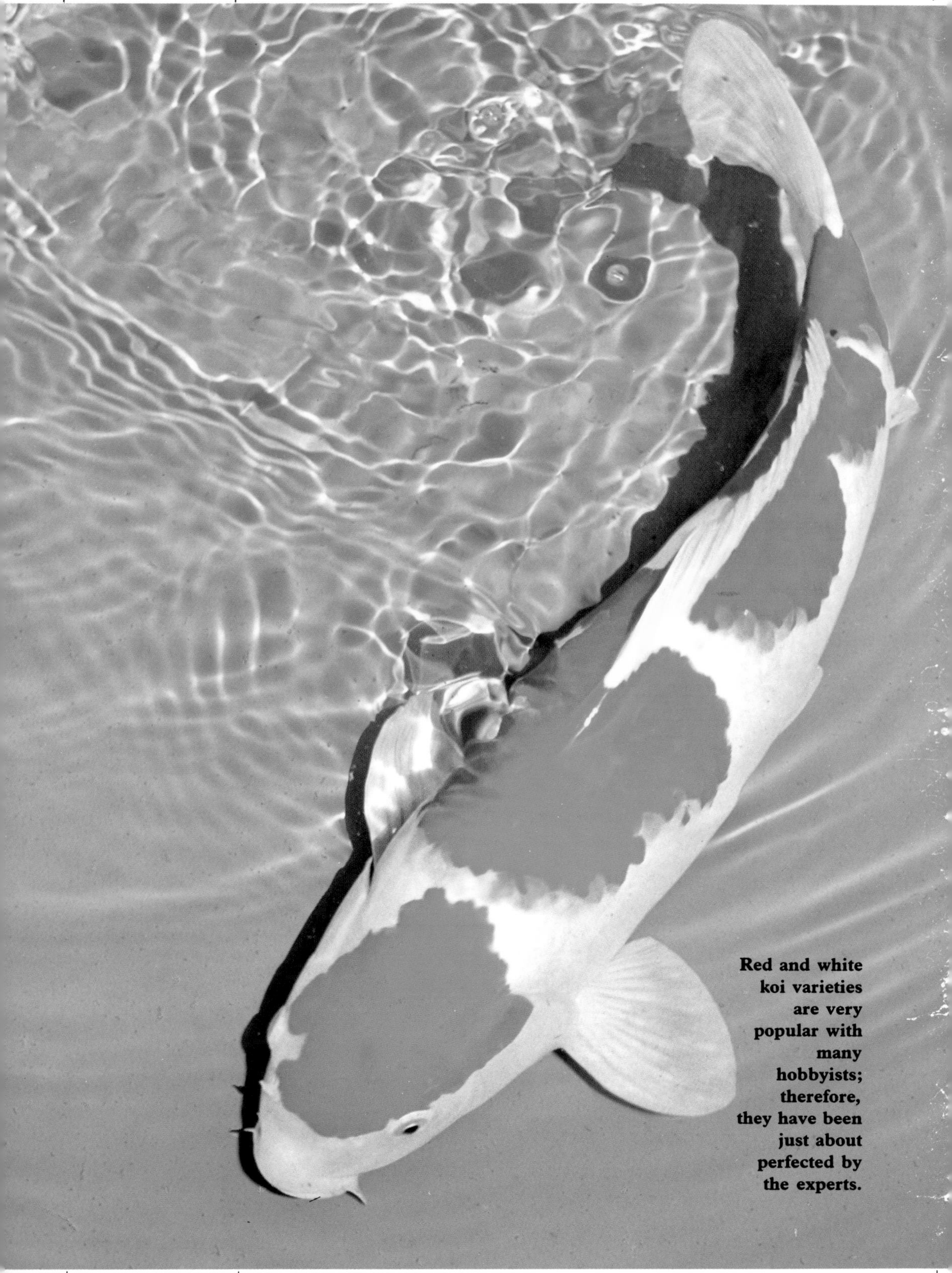

Red and white
koi varieties
are very
popular with
many
hobbyists;
therefore,
they have been
just about
perfected by
the experts.

Kage showa koi. Note the leather-like look of this fish.

be available at all times as this is a crucial developmental stage. Infusoria, microscopic unicellular organisms, can be cultivated. Brine shrimp cultures purchased at petshops make excellent food for fry. A dim light over the rearing tank at night encourages the fry to continue eating. Their growth will be quicker.

Dry pellet foods can be introduced when the fry are four to six weeks old. Continue to maintain a high protein diet to guarantee maximum growth potential.

SIZE. The fry are about 6 mm (¼ in) long when hatched. They add to their size at the rate of 6 mm per week over the first few weeks. The rate of growth is affected by a variety of factors, but by one year of age the average koi is 10 cm (4 in). Growth will be continual in koi raised in climates that are warm year

'round. Growth will cease in the late fall and resume in the spring in more northerly countries.

Koi have a hormone growth inhibitor when confronted with overcrowded conditions. Give them as much room as possible. Aeration may be beneficial, also. Older, established colors, such as kohaku, are likely to be the most rapid growers.

CULLING. Culling should be done as soon as any

"A dim light over the rearing tank encourages the fry to continue eating. Their growth will be quicker."

Tancho showa, or red-patched, koi. Tancho koi are sometimes called red-crested koi.

deformed fish are noticed. These fish can be placed in a container of ice cubes. Or they can be fed to the adult koi. This may seem cruel, but remember that nature allows only the fittest to survive. The breeder must equate natural selection in a domestic environment.

The rearing of substandard

improve one feature, another may suffer. Therefore, breeding is a compromise between many aspects.

Two strategies can be used. First, you can concentrate on obtaining excellence in one particular feature. When this has been achieved, you can breed for another feature. Alternatively, your goal can

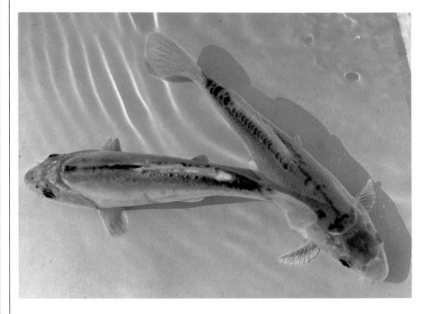

Kinshu, or golden metallic mirror, koi. This variety is also known as embroidered brocade.

"The rearing of substandard koi results in a negative effect on the whole koi population. These fish invariably are more prone to disease and have declining breeding ability."

koi results in a negative effect on the koi population as a whole. These fish invariably are more prone to disease and have declining breeding ability.

GENETICS. The genetic aspects of koi are complex. The novice breeder should know a few basics, though.

Overall shape, coloring, patterns and scale type are all inherited independent of one another. In an attempt to

be to raise the overall standards on a continuum. This means slower progress on any one feature. The important thing with either strategy is to carefully think it through.

The only way to know the genotype (non-visual genetic make-up) of a fish is to monitor all the phenotypes (external appearances) of the offspring. Over time you will be able to make sound

Koshinishiki, a variety of the taisho sanshoku or three-step tricolor koi. Note the three red patches or steps on this fish.

inferences about the genetic state. There are books on fish genetics.

Do not introduce any fish of unknown heritage once you have a good breeding stock. Introducing genes to an established stock complicates matters. Remember that genes control every aspect of a koi, including predisposition to illness and breeding vigor. Once your stock shows steady improvement, purchase extra stock that specifically will improve a given feature. Do not introduce new fish in a haphazard fashion.

"Do not produce any fish of unknown heritage once you have a good breeding stock. Introducing genes to an established stock complicates matters."

Yamatonishiki, another variety of the taisho sanshoku. This particular koi has too much red, causing the three red steps run together. Breeding well-marked koi is not easy but is certainly a challenge.

Exhibitions

Koi exhibitions are a highly organized business in Japan and getting that way in the rest of the world. The shows range from small to very large. The prizes vary from moderate to magnificent. A top winning koi can command a substantial fee if its owner decides to sell it.

Things are less grand outside of Japan. Shows are still in their infancy in most countries. It is an aspect of the hobby that grows steadily in its supporters each year.

The shows are organized by various koi societies. They may be indoor or outdoor. The koi are usually exhibited in blue plastic pools. These are usually circular with a diameter of 1.8–3 m (6–10 ft). Classes are based on sizes ranging from 15 cm (6 in), in steps of 10 cm (4 in), to koi over 56

Koi body shapes: 1) wild body type; 2) show body type; 3) modified wild body type; 4) deep body type. Body type is becoming increasingly important in exhibition koi.

"There are classes for different colors and patterns. The koi are judged by experienced owners and breeders on a point system."

cm (22 in).

There are classes for different colors and patterns. The koi are judged by experienced owners and breeders on a point system.

Only one or two fish in a vat are selected for closer examination. They are put in plastic crates. In Japan, the koi often are transferred to large aquariums so they can be evaluated better. These judges take into account features not seen easily from an overhead position.

You must be a member of your national koi society or the society organizing the show to be eligible to enter your koi. The show secretary provides entry forms and show rules. All forms must be completed carefully. Incorrect information results in automatic disqualification in most shows.

Membership is recommended even if you do not participate in a show. You will receive newsletters on club activities and articles on all aspects of koi ownership.

SHOW QUALITY. The standards of quality vary not only from country to country, but from show to

J.R.QUINN

show. As expected, the world's best koi are found in Japan. While winners are exported
the best koi remain with the Japanese breeders.

LENGTH AND WEIGHT. The object is not simply to produce a large, heavy fish. Overall shape, color and markings are more important. As a rule of thumb, a show koi should not exceed the following length-to-weight measurements:

60 cm and over: 5–12 kg (11–26 lb.)

50–60 cm (20–24 in): 2–7.5

kg (4.4–16.5 lb.)
36–50 cm (14–20 in)

COLOR AND MARKINGS. It is essential that the color be as even as possible and cover the entire fish, in a single colored koi. However, in red the color does not always extend to the tips of the fins. This color often changes to either a more orange shade or a deeper red.

The red in kohakus must be vivid and dense. The number of color steps should be distinct, balanced and sharply contrasted against the white. The white must be pure. No speckles of red or any other intrusions should be present on it. If the white is anything less, it does not matter how good the red markings are. The fins should be white, though a hint of pink is often noticeable.

The markings are variable in sanshoku varieties. The white should be pure and the red as intense as possible.

The black should be dense, not faded or blue-brown. It is permissible for black streaks to extend into the fins.

The best effect in the tancho sanke are sufficient black markings. Otherwise the koi looks mismarked rather than striking. Often the white is spoiled by brown and blue intrusions. The showa sanke should have

bold areas of black and red. If little white is present, it is termed hi showa.

The main problem of the utsuri colors is retaining the black in a solid mass without its speckling the second color. The aka (red) and ki (yellow) bekko koi must have a balance between the black and the other color that is neither under- nor overstressed. Dappled black spotting is undesirable.

Patterning should be cleanly demarcated. In the case of matsuba pattern, examples with clear heads are more striking than heads blotched with color. The pine cone effect should be constant over the entire dorsal surface without being interrupted by the contrasting body color. Doitsu scaled fish should have the mirror-like scales in even rows. Missing scales spoil the effect.

The beginner koi exhibitor is advised to show well-established colors and patterns first. Once familiar with these, exhibiting the more unusual varieties can be attempted. By this time you will be aware of the complex standards demanded of these fish.

"The beginner koi exhibitor is advised to show well-established colors and patterns first. Once familiar with these, exhibiting the more unusual varieties can be attempted."

Taisho sanshoku, or three-step tricolor, koi. Note the wonderful condition of this fish.

Health

The most important factor in maintaining healthy koi is to devote a great deal of attention to the quality of the water. Many problems are attributable to the failure of creating a balanced state in the pond.

It is not possible to rid a pond of all disease organisms. The presence of these organisms in controlled amounts allows the fish to develop a resistance to them. A fish develops immunity to illness by being exposed to it in small doses. A fish never exposed to a given organism is more likely to succumb to it. Species of fish vary in their resistance to specific bacteria, fungi and parasites.

These comments apply to the disease as well. If a given

"It is not possible to rid a pond of all disease organisms. The presence of these organisms in controlled amounts allows the fish to develop a resistance to them."

bacteria is exposed to a low level of lethal treatment, it develops a resistance to it. The further use of this treatment is futile. Some bacteria are more virulent than others, so a remedy that worked well on one occasion may have little effect at a later date.

The very treatments that kill disease organisms are no less dangerous to the koi. The koi survive because they are able to withstand the dosage levels that destroy most unicellular bacteria and parasites. However, the treatment may lower the koi's overall health. They may be more susceptible to attack by other organisms. This is why it is important not to overuse a remedy.

Often illness is not of a single cause. Therefore, two separate treatments may be required. Sometimes the remedies may be offered together, sometimes they must be taken one at a time. Treat the more dangerous condition first.

Some thought must be given as to whether to treat an individual fish or to treat the pond as a whole. At times it is best to remove all the fish from the pool and replace the water. As you can see, it is much simpler to prevent disease than it is to treat it.

Disease is kept in check in many ways in the wild. Fish have numerous defense mechanisms, ranging from the mucus secretion over the

Artist's rendering of raised scales on a koi. Raised scales are a typical symptom of dropsy. A dropsical fish will also be quite bloated.

Artist's rendering of a koi afflicted with *Epistylis*. Symptoms include loss of appetite and general listlessness. As for most piscine diseases, the best cure for this is prevention.

scales to antibodies that engulf alien organisms within the body. Harmful bacteria are not able to multiply to high levels in a given stretch of water because the water is constantly moving. A less than fit wild fish is devoured by one of the many carnivorous lifeforms, such as other fish, mammals, birds and reptiles. Rarely does a fish develop an illness to the same extent that it

Creating an overcrowded pond is akin to asking for an epidemic. Keep in mind that once one fish gets sick, the odds are pretty good that its pondmates will, too.

"A volume of water is as much a unit for breeding disease as it is for keeping fish. It can reasonably be inferred that all fish in a pond are infected if an illness is visible on one koi."

might in a domestic situation; a delicate balance exists between all lifeforms. Natural selection insures that each species of life is propagated only by those most fit.

BREEDING DISEASE

A volume of water is as much a unit for breeding disease as it is for keeping fish. It can reasonably be inferred that all fish in a pond are infected if an illness is visible on one koi. How quickly an illness spreads is determined by how vigilant the owner is about checking the fish and restoring the balance of the pool.

Poor husbandry is

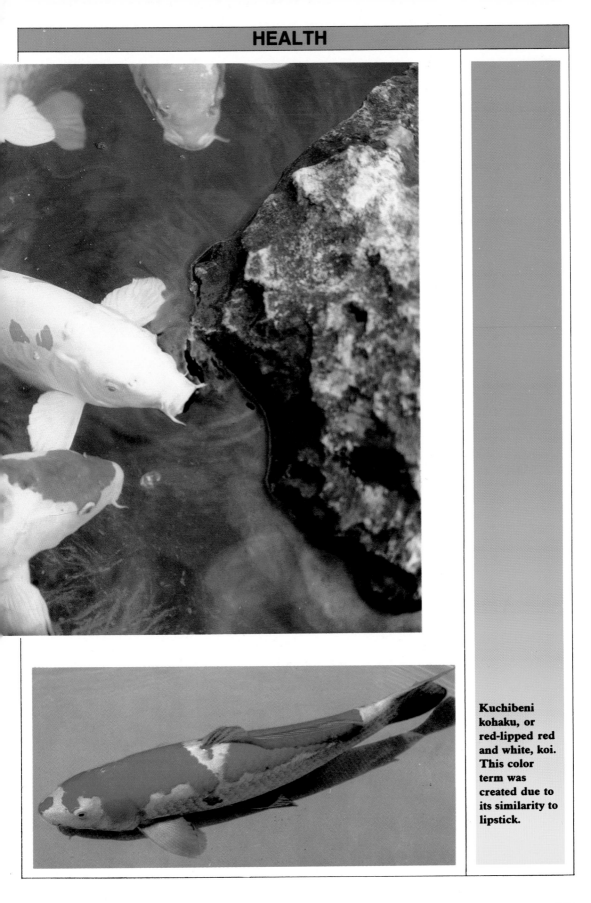

Kuchibeni kohaku, or red-lipped red and white, koi. This color term was created due to its similarity to lipstick.

"Polluted water as a result of overfeeding provides an ideal habitat for bacteria."

Artist's rendering of a koi with myxosporidia, or whirling disease. This disease is probably caused by the ingestion of an infected tubifex worm.

probably the greatest cause of illness in a koi pond. Most matters are basically under the control of the pondkeeper. Proper technique is normally sufficient to keep the pool inhabitants healthy. The following are conditions in which disease and fungus multiply rapidly:

1. LACK OF WATER CIRCULATION. Stagnant or slow moving water is a prime medium for bacteria.

2. LACK OF WATER REPLACEMENT. Replacing a percentage of water on a regular basis dilutes the ratio of bacteria to water. Harmful organisms are kept in check.

3. OVERCROWDING. Micro-organisms have no difficulty in finding a suitable host when the conditions are overcrowded.

4. UNSUITABLE WATER CONDITIONS. Polluted water as a result of overfeeding provides an ideal habitat for bacteria. Less obvious states of unsuitability fall under this heading, also. For example,

a fish transferred from one water supply to another of differing pH is stressed. Always adjust water conditions in a holding tank over a period of time to equate that of the final home.

5. STRESS. Along with water condition, this is the most common inducer of fish disease. It is a state that cannot be seen visually. Certain conditions, though, are sure to create stress. Avoid or minimize stress situations.

6. INADEQUATE NUTRITION. Poor nutrition weakens a fish's internal defense mechanisms.

Artist's rendering of a koi with gill rot. This is a fungal disease which reduces the blood supply to the gills; in turn, the gill tissue "rots" due to the lack of oxygenated blood.

Asagi, or blue, koi, also known as the pale blue koi.

"A fish in an advanced state of disease is not difficult to recognize. The tricky aspect is noticing a problem at an early stage."

Gin, or silver metallic, showa koi.

7. INJURY. Secondary infection is likely to strike an injured koi. Treat problems promptly.

RECOGNIZING POOR HEALTH

A fish in an advanced state of disease is not difficult to recognize. The tricky aspect is noticing a problem at an early stage. This is possible only if the owner spends a lot of time observing his fish and is able to notice any changes.

Lack of eating is one of the earliest signs of illness. A

Kikusui, a variety of the shusui or mirror koi, which has wavy orange patterns.

"Loss of appetite in an established fish should prompt the owner to suspect a problem. The koi should be removed to an isolation tank, if you can catch it!"

Yamabuki hariwake, or pale yellow white metallic, koi.

newly acquired koi may take a day or two to begin feeding. This is of no concern. Loss of appetite in an established fish should prompt the owner to suspect a problem. The koi should be removed to an isolation tank, if you can catch it!

A fish that is listless yet otherwise appears sound is another candidate for monitoring. The fish may be resting, or it may be showing an early sign of poor health.

A koi with sudden and erratic movements or that rubs against rocks is suffering from an ailment. A healthy koi does not attempt to scratch itself. White, brown, gray or black spots on a fish indicate a problem. A koi panting near the surface may have a gill ailment.

Swellings or scales raised above their normal lie need attention. A koi having difficulty maintaining its position in the water or

A variety of medicines and water treatments are available at your local aquarium or pet shop. Some are designed to treat a specific illness or eradicate a specific pest, while others have more broad-based applications. Photo courtesy of Aquarium Products.

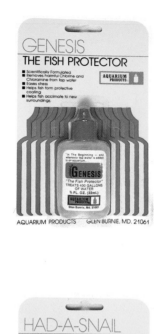

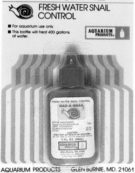

"A quarantine tank should be large enough to allow a fish to move about. Ideally, only one fish should be kept per tank."

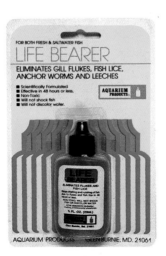

swimming at an angle is ill. Skin lesions are also a matter of concern. Read a book about fish diseases or discuss it at your local petshop.

ISOLATION TANK

A quarantine tank should be large enough to allow a fish to move about. Ideally, only one fish should be kept per tank. A small airstone provides aeration. Nothing more than a simple foam filter is required. Sterilized gravel may be added, but it is not essential. Do not include any live plants. Plastic plants or a few rocks may be offered to give the koi a sense of security. This reduces the risk of the fish being stressed.

Add 3 gm per liter (2¾ teaspoons per gallon) of household salt and 3–4 mg per liter of malachite green. These are excellent

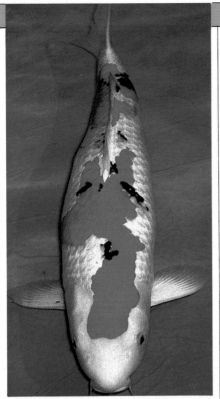

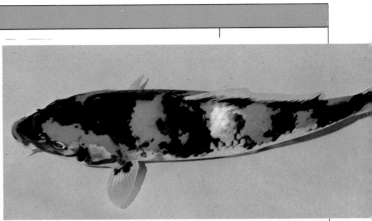

pond. Float the transport bag of the fish in the isolation tank to equalize the water temperatures. After an hour, carefully take the koi from the transport bag by hand and place it in the tank.

therapeutic chemicals. They successfully control low levels of many potentially harmful organisms. Other water conditioners are available at your local petshop. It is important to know the exact volume of water in the tank. This is vital in administering accurate dosages of remedies.

Equate the pH level of the isolation tank to that of the Do not introduce any of the water in the bag into the tank. If the fish is harboring an ailment, the transport water will be teeming with bacteria. Do not feed the fish for 24 hours.

The isolation period should be from 10 to 21 days. Before re-introducing the fish to its regular home, equalize the water temperature of the tank to that of the pond.

TREATING ILLNESS

A koi may be treated for any injury or illness in several ways. Much depends on the nature of the ailment, such as whether it is present on a single fish or throughout the pond.

A physical injury involving an open wound, ulcers or other skin lesion must be treated on an individual basis in isolation. A single fish showing signs of illness again needs attention. A general medication may also be added to the pond water. If a number of koi exhibit signs of disease, isolate the worst affected to quarantine tanks. Treat the rest of the fish in the pond.

Do not treat fish without the advice of an experienced keeper. Incorrect diagnosis and treatment often result in death of the koi. Other important points must be considered:

1. If the koi vary widely in size, the smaller fish should be removed. They cannot cope with the same dosage of remedies as can the larger fish.

2. Other species of fish in the pond may not be able to withstand the same dosage levels as the adult koi. They may have to be removed to another tank.

3. Chemicals in medicines

inactivate biological filters. They kill the beneficial bacteria. Activated charcoal in filters inactivate medicines. Therefore, filtration systems must be switched off when treating a pool. Mechanical filters with by-pass pipes may be employed.

4. It may be better to remove all the fish from the pond if parasites and other organisms difficult to eradicate are present. Also remove all plants. Disinfect the pond with large quantities of chlorine. Fill and empty the pond until all the chlorine has been removed.

Top: **Taisho sanshoku, or three-step tricolor, koi.** *Bottom:* **Kohaku, or red and white, koi.**

"It may be better to remove all the fish from the pond if parasites and other organisms difficult to eradicate are present."

Suggested Reading

DR. AXELROD'S ATLAS OF FRESHWATER AQUARIUM FISHES

By Dr. Herbert R. Axelrod and others

TFH H-1077

Here is a truly beautiful and immensely colorful book that satisfies the long-existing need for a *comprehensive* identification guide to aquarium fishes that find their way onto world markets. This book describes and depicts in full-color not only the popular aquarium fishes but also the oddballs and weirdos, not just the warmwater species but the coldwater fishes as well. However, not all of

Taisho sanshoku, or three-step tricolor, koi.

Kohaku, or red and white, koi.

this beautiful text/photo package is concerned with identification and maintenance alone. In addition to showing the fishes and telling exactly what they are, this volume also provides information—plus step-by-step full-color photographic sequences—about the spawning of a number of species from different families.

KOI VARIETIES: JAPANESE COLORED CARP-NISHIKIGOI
By Dr. Herbert R. Axelrod
ISBN 0-86622-885-3
TFH PS-875

This colorful book covers the many available varieties, selection, and history of the increasingly popular koi. Included in this book are sections concerning real and artificial coloring in koi, keeping koi, long-finned and pygmy koi, and many others. Especially helpful to the avid breeder or pond owner who wants specialized information about these prized fish, this volume also contains a revealing section about the genetics of koi.

GOLDFISH AND KOI IN YOUR HOME
By Dr. Herbert R. Axelrod and William Vorderwinkler
ISBN 0-86622-041-0
TFH H-909

This volume is written especially for the home aquarium and tropical fish hobbyist. It contains complete data on care

Sanshoku, or tricolor, koi.

and feeding, treatment of fish diseases, water conditions, and everything necessary for the home owner of goldfish and koi. Additionally, this volume contains chapters on choosing proper aquarium plants and setting up the garden pool.

KOI AND GARDEN PONDS: A COMPLETE INTRODUCTION
By Dr. Herbert R. Axelrod
Hardcover: ISBN 0-86622-398-3; TFH CO-040
Softcover: ISBN 0-86622-399-1; TFH CO-040S

This book is for anyone interested in the colorful Japanese carp and for owners of garden pools. This is a truly beautiful book with great value, especially as a guide for identification of the many different scale and color patterns of koi.

GARDEN PONDS: A COMPLETE INTRODUCTION
By Al David
Hardcover: ISBN 0-86622-266-9; TFH CO-017
Softcover: ISBN 0-86622-298-7; TFH CO-017S

This highly colorful book, completely illustrated with full-color photographs and line drawings, shows and tells the reader how to go about setting up a garden pond or pool. Authoritative advice is given about making the pond, how to protect it against enemies, which fish and plants to put into it—and how to keep it beautiful!

JOHN DAWES'S BOOK OF WATER GARDENS
By John Dawes
ISBN 0-86622-662-1
TFH H-1104

A comprehensive text

designed to answer all your queries about garden ponds, this book touches all the bases. For the novice and the connoisseur, this book lays the foundation to a successful garden pond and provides a practical approach for its beautiful completion. Whether you live in a southern, northern, or temperate climate; whether you inhabit a large estate or reside in a garden; apartment whether you wish to enhance your garden decor, closely study pond plants and fishes, or simply start a garden pond from scratch, this beautifully illustrated, easily readable and straightforward volume has all the answers.

WATER GARDENS FOR PLANTS AND FISH
By Charles B. Thomas
ISBN 0-86622-942-6
TFH TS-102

Whether you are a novice or a seasoned water gardener, you will find in this book priceless information detailing everything you will ever need to know to create a wonderful, uniquely beautiful water garden of your own. The water gardening secrets of several generations of leaders in the

development of the science of water lily culture are generously shared with you by the author. Over 200 full-color photographs and illustrations identify scores of lilies, lotuses, accessory aquatic plants, fishes, aquatic animals, and established private gardens.

Nidan kohaku, or two-step red and white, koi.

Illustration Index

Index

INDEX

INDEX